PATH FOR GREATNESS:
WORK AS SPIRITUAL SERVICE

Linda J. Ferguson

Trafford Publishing

Excerpts from *The Words of Martin Luther King Jr.*, selected by Coretta Scott King,
published by Newmarket Press, 1983. Used with permission of the King Estate and
the Writers House, LLC.

Extracted from *Take Your Soul to Work* by Tanis Helliwell. Copyright © 1999.
Reprinted by permission of Random House Canada, division of Random House of
Canada Limited.

From *The Art of Happiness - A Handbook for the Living* by Dalai Lama and
Howard C. Cutler, copyright © 1998 by H H Dalai Lama and Howard C. Cutler.
Used by permission of Putnam Berkley, a division of Penguin Putnam Inc.

Story of the river creatures from *Illusions: The Adventures of a Reluctant
Messiah*, by Richard Bach, copyright © 1977. Used with permission of
Dell Publishing, a division of Random House Inc.

Story of Jumping Mouse from *Seven Arrows* by Hyemeyohsts Storm, copyright © 1972 by
Hyemeyohsts Storm. Used by permission of HarperCollins Publishers, Inc.

Quote from *The Invitation* by Oriah Mountain Dreamer, copyright 1999 by Oriah Mountain
Dreamer. Used by permission of Oriah Mountain Dreamer and HarperCollins Publishers Inc.

Story of Joel's Day in *Living, Loving, and Learning* by Leo F. Buscaglia.
Permission granted by Steven Short for LFB, Inc.

Lyrics from *Find the Spirit* by the Washington Sisters, used with permission of
Sändra Washington. Copyright © 1987.

Canadian Cataloguing in Publication Data

Ferguson, Linda J., 1961-
  Path for greatness

  Includes bibliographical references.
  ISBN 1-55212-498-3

  1. Work--Religious aspects. 2. Self-actualization
(Psychology)--Religious aspects. 3. Spiritual life. I. Title.
BL65.W67F47 2000   291.4   C00-911179-4

TRAFFORD

This book was published *on-demand* in cooperation with Trafford Publishing.
On-demand publishing is a unique process and service of making a book available for retail
sale to the public taking advantage of on-demand manufacturing and Internet marketing.
On-demand publishing includes promotions, retail sales, manufacturing, order fulfillment,
accounting and collecting royalties on behalf of the author.

Suite 6E, 2333 Government St., Victoria, B.C. V8T 4P4, CANADA
Phone   250-383-6864   Toll-free   1-888-232-4444 (Canada & US)
Fax   250-383-6804   E-mail   sales@trafford.com
Web site   www.trafford.com   TRAFFORD PUBLISHING IS A DIVISION OF TRAFFORD HOLDINGS LTD.
Trafford Catalogue #00-0163   www.trafford.com/robots/00-0163.html

10   9   8

CONTENTS

ACKNOWLEDGEMENTS IX

INTRODUCTION 1

THE VALUE OF WORKING SPIRITUALLY 1

Organization of Book 3

Goals for this Book 4

Crossing Language Barriers 5

Closing Remarks 6

PART I PATH FOR GREATNESS 7

CHAPTER 1: WORK AS SPIRITUAL SERVICE 9

CULTIVATING YOUR SPIRITUAL VALUES AND PRINCIPLES 11

STORIES OF GREATNESS 13

Sharing Her Gifts 13

Troubadour of Greatness 16

Table for 6 Billion Please 18

BOULDERS ALONG THE SPIRITUAL PATH 20

CHAPTER 2: FINDING YOUR PURPOSE IN VOCATION 22

RIGHT LIVELIHOOD 24

VOCATION AS A CALLING 24

Discovering My Higher Purpose 28

Enter the Darkness 31

EXERCISES 34

CHAPTER 3: USING YOUR GIFTS: SHARING
    YOUR PASSION 36
    ENTREPRENEURS AND ARTISTS USE THEIR GIFTS 37
    SHARING YOUR PASSION 40
    USING THE GIFT OF COMPASSION 41
    GETTING PAST LEARNED LIMITATIONS 43
    EXERCISES 48
CHAPTER 4: THE SPIRITUALITY OF WORK 49
    SPIRITUAL MEANING OF WORK 51
    SPIRITUALITY VS. RELIGION 53
        Working Spiritually *54*
        Work Spiritually or Wither on the Vine *57*
    EXERCISES 59

PART II BRINGING SPIRITUALITY
TO YOUR WORK 61

CHAPTER 5: CREATING NEW METAPHORS 63
    METAPHORS AS MENTAL MODELS 63
        Spiritual Metaphors *66*
        Metaphors in Stories *69*
        Childhood Metaphors *71*
        Alternative Metaphors for Work and Organizations *73*
        Metaphors for Organizations *76*
    EXERCISES 80
CHAPTER 6: AFFECTING CHANGE: "LIVING AS IF" 81
    THE POWER OF VISION 86
    BEING PRESENT TO THE NEGATIVES 89
    EXERCISES 94
CHAPTER 7: LIVING INTENTIONALLY 96
    LIVING INTENTIONALLY AS CO-CREATORS 98
    LIVING INTENTIONALLY AS MINDFULNESS 102
    AND NOW A WORD ABOUT LOVE 106
    EXERCISES 112
CHAPTER 8: SPIRITUAL GUIDANCE 113
    OPENING UP TO GUIDANCE 114
    BEING VULNERABLE 118

INTUITION AND DISCERNMENT 121

EXERCISES 124

CHAPTER 9: CREATING SACRED SPACE,
CREATING SACRED TIME 125

CREATING SACRED SPACE 126

CREATING SACRED TIME 130

SACRIFICIAL COMMITMENTS 134

EXERCISES 137

CHAPTER 10: HEALING FROM ADDICTIONS 138

CHARACTERISTICS OF ADDICTION 140

CO-DEPENDENCY 145

WORK AS ADDICTION; ORGANIZATIONS AS ADDICTS 147

EXERCISES 151

PART III WORKING SPIRITUALLY

WITH OTHERS 153

CHAPTER 11: SACRED TRUST 155

INGREDIENTS OF TRUST 155

MAINTAINING TRUST 158

TURF GUARDING AND SCARCITY VS. SHARING
  AND ABUNDANCE 162

EXERCISES 165

CHAPTER 12: TEAMWORK: SPIRIT OF THE WHOLE 167

TEAMWORK WITH DIFFICULT PEOPLE
  (A.K.A., ANGELS-IN-TRAINING) 170

TAKING RESPONSIBILITY 173

PARTNERSHIP VS. SUPERIORITY 176

RELATIONSHIPS VS. HEIRARCHY 177

SPIRITUALLY-GROUNDED GROUP DECISION-MAKING 178

EXERCISES 183

CHAPTER 13: SEXUALITY AND SPIRITUALITY 186

UNDERSTANDING FEAR AND LOVE 186

EXPRESSING EMOTIONS AT WORK 188

SEXUALITY AND SPIRITUALITY 189

AND NOW A WORD ABOUT SEXUAL HARASSMENT 193

EXERCISES 195

CHAPTER 14: ANGER AND RECONCILIATION **196**
RETRIEVING THE GIFT FROM YOUR ANGER AND FEARS 196
GROUP AND ORGANIZATIONAL HEALING 201
RECONCILIATION AS HEALING WORK 205
FINDING THE GIFTS IN OTHERS' SHORTCOMINGS 208
EXERCISES 212

CHAPTER 15: ORGANIZATIONAL RITUALS AND
RITES OF PASSAGE **214**
CULTURE AND RITUALS 215
RITES OF PASSAGE 220
ORGANIZATIONAL RITES OF PASSAGE 222
SUMMARY 228
EXERCISES 230

PART IV ORGANIZATIONS AS ARENAS FOR SPIRITUAL GROWTH 233

CHAPTER 16: NEW VS. OLD PARADIGMS **235**
CHANGING VIEWS OF EMPLOYEES THROUGHOUT THE
TWENTIETH CENTURY 237
WORKING SPIRITUALLY IN TRADITIONAL ORGANIZATIONS 242
PARADIGM SHIFT 243
ABUNDANCE AND OPPORTUNITY 246
TRUTHFUL COMMUNITY 249
EXERCISES 252

CHAPTER 17: BECOMING A HIGHER CONSCIOUSNESS
ORGANIZATION **253**
WHY BECOME A HIGHER CONSCIOUSNESS ORGANIZATION? 253
BASIC PREMISES OF HIGHER CONSCIOUSNESS ORGANIZATIONS 256
BECOMING A HIGHER CONSCIOUSNESS ORGANIZATION 258
HOW HIGHER CONSCIOUSNESS ORGANIZATIONS OPERATE: 260
PERSONAL GROWTH IS TOP PRIORITY 263
PERFORMANCE REVIEWS, PROMOTIONS, AND TRANSITIONS 264
TRUST AND TEAMWORK 266
VISION AND LEADERSHIP 268
SOUTHWEST AIRLINES DEMONSTRATES A NEW WAY TO WORK 270

CONTENTS

SUMMARY 275
EXERCISES 276

BIBLIOGRAPHY 277
ENDNOTES 283
ABOUT THE AUTHOR 289

Martin, Marla Baker, Tracy deLuca, Ellen Valentine, Elizabeth Stadig, Dick Hawkins, Mary Ann Macklin, David Barnes, Jeff Jones and Bill Linden.

Thanks goes as well to my local ASTD chapter (Valleys of Virginia ASTD) and Hollins University for several travel grants to attend spirituality and work conferences over the past three years. These conferences provided new contacts and experiences that expanded my thinking.

To my editor, Kerry Mead, I owe my gratitude for her diligence and thoughtful questions to help me present my ideas more clearly. I would also like to thank Jennie Isbell for her thorough editorial assistance in the final manuscript review.

Thanks goes to Marla Baker at AmGraph Design and Azurae Windwalker for their work on the book cover. I also want to thank the various staff at Trafford Publishing for their assistance getting this book to the public in a timely and professional manner.

I can't offer a big enough thanks to my circle of friends over the past few years who have kept this book in their hearts and prayers. I must offer here my heartfelt gratitude for your continued love for me and belief in me to complete this project. So as not to omit someone- You all know who you are.

Finally, I must acknowledge those people who have helped me grow and excel during critical periods in my life. To my family, teachers, and mentors, you have left your mark on me and I am blessed.

INTRODUCTION

Everybody can be great because anybody can serve.

— Martin Luther King, Jr.

THE VALUE OF WORKING SPIRITUALLY

Imagine having a sense of personal wholeness, meaning, and connection in your work. How differently would you feel if you worked in that manner? My guess is your personal greatness would shine through your work if you did. One way to follow your path for greatness is to focus on your spiritual growth through work. We spend most of our waking hours at work. Thus it is essential we find ways to bring spirituality to our work so we grow to our fullest potential. This book provides ideas for personal spiritual growth that will lead you on your journey for greatness.

Often it is in our work that we find the best opportunities for spiritual growth to take place. Through encounters with co-workers we have the opportunity to be more compassionate, understanding, accepting and forgiving. In seeing our work as loving service, we develop ourselves as spiritual beings.

As the global market place forces organizations to be more competitive, often resulting in companies producing more with fewer people, one of the distinguishing features between a well run organization and one that flounders will be the creativity, motivation and cooperation of the workforce. People who work spiritually are those who see themselves serving a greater purpose through their work, who see the spiritual value of working with others, and who have a stronger spiritual foundation to cope with increasing demands.

For those people who have little to no control of how their work is structured or conducted, the frustration can be enormous. In these situations people are looking for ways that their job can be less stressful and more tolerable, if not even more joyful and more meaningful. Working from a spiritual base helps people learn how to cope with changing circumstances and stressful conditions. Working spiritually allows people to see how they can grow through their work and how they can shift their attitudes towards work.

It is essential we see our work life as a place to follow our spiritual journey. The focus of this book is on growing spiritually to find and live our greatness. To live our greatness doesn't necessarily mean we must accomplish great things, only that we live true to who we are, offering our best gifts and passion to the world in service. It is the spirit and intention with which we do our work that determines whether our greatness shines forth.

Many of the stories in this book about working spiritually may seem rather ordinary. Indeed, seeing the sacred in ordinary day to day living is part of following a spiritual path.

Working spiritually involves a holistic perspective of how we live and work. We must not separate our lives so that we are spiritual only on the weekends. Our spirituality grows when it becomes one continuous flow in our life.

ORGANIZATION OF BOOK

Part I outlines a framework for seeing how your work is a path for spiritual greatness. Part II provides ideas for strengthening your spiritual practice in your work. I describe how to create new metaphors for work, find your right livelihood, and be intentionally spiritual. By doing so, you will find greater meaning for what you do and bring the fullest of who you are to your work and organization. Part III focuses on ways to work spiritually with others. It includes ways to bring forth your gifts and create greater awareness to enhance teamwork, group processes, and meetings. The chapters on teamwork and organizational rituals examine how we work spiritually as a group or collective. Exercises are provided at the end of most chapters to help you practice the ideas presented.

Part IV outlines a new paradigm for organizations based on the premise that organizations are arenas in which people's personal spiritual journeys take place. By being intentionally spiritual at work, and bringing our personal greatness to our work, we help our organizations become more spiritual places. It is time to call for the creation of "Higher Consciousness Organizations" – organizations that believe in all people's quest for wholeness, meaning, and connection. Teams, departments, and entire organizations can be intentional about supporting members' spiritual growth. Throughout this book I provide examples of organizations that believe they must be intentional about developing their people.

One difference between this book and others that address the issue of spirituality at work is my discussion of the organizational influences that shape our individual spiritual journey. If we want to work fully spiritually, organizations must support our spiritual growth. It is through dialogue and relationships with others that we discover more about ourselves. In our daily work encounters, we travel further along our spiritual path by being in relation with one another in more authentic and compassionate ways.

Goals for this Book

I want to briefly explain my purpose and process of writing this book. My purpose for doing this book comes from my desire to propose another way of working, a way that leaves people feeling fulfilled rather than empty, enriched rather than drained, affirmed rather than angry. We must focus on growing spiritually during our daily work to live our personal greatness.

Like so many others, I have a strong yearning to bring my wholeness of being into alignment with my work. The task of writing this book has been a challenge for me to work spiritually, to keep open to guidance and inner clarity as I struggle to find the right words to put on the page. My process of living in the moment with my work – being both task-oriented and spiritually aware – provided me the experience of living what I was writing.

The focus of this book is on service in your vocation. However, since volunteerism in community groups is an important way to develop greatness through loving service, I hope the ideas will be applied to work in civic groups and other places where people combine their talent and efforts for a greater good. When we understand that our life quest is to grow spiritually, we can live this quest through the myriad of experiences that allow us to be more compassionate and loving, anywhere and at any time we choose. That is the ultimate in living a spiritually great life. I invite you to enter this book from whatever point along your spiritual path you are.

CROSSING LANGUAGE BARRIERS

The ideas presented in this book build on numerous views regarding spirituality and work. Many modern and ancient writers have reflected on how work is an essential part of spiritual development, as well as how life can be more spiritual through work. I reference such writers to demonstrate the diversity of ideas on this topic and to acknowledge their work.

Since this book bridges ideas from various writings on spirituality and management, it creates challenges for language usage. Because people will encounter the ideas of this book from different spiritual and/or organizational perspectives, it is a challenge to anticipate how different people will react to words related to working spiritually.

Words such as compassion, authenticity, awareness or trust may be easy to accept as workplace language, whereas words such as forgiveness, mindfulness, atonement, or love may be harder for some people to use at work. Because there are so many interpretations and characterizations of a divine power, I want to be explicit in how I am referring to such a power here. Words that are capitalized throughout the book refer to the Abiding, Abundant Love that goes by many names, yet is beyond naming. This is done in recognition that one word for this Source is too limiting.

I use language from various faith traditions so that people will understand the universality of the concepts presented. I use stories from various faith traditions to show that working spiritually isn't based on one belief system or connected to any singular religious doctrine. It is important that people understand the distinction I make in chapter 4 between spirituality and religion. I hope to reclaim some traditionally "religious" words as universal human characteristics so they can be used at work and in organizations.

Finally, references to personal pronouns will be varied such that "he" may be used in one sentence and "she" in the next. The intent behind this is to be as inclusive as possible and to avoid focusing on one gender exclusively when making a point. The process of working spiritually transcends gender.

CLOSING REMARKS

I hope you will find a message in this book that resonates with you so that you too can work spiritually and live your personal greatness. As we become intentional about our spiritual journey, we can be beacons for others who want to follow a spiritual path. Following such a path is not easy. However, the rewards from living your authentic self through your work will be worth the hardships.

This book is meant as a catalyst for other books and deeper conversation on this topic, not as a be-all end-all text. You are invited to explore, to question, to experiment with these ideas in the hope that you will be able to experience your wholeness of being and connectedness with others as well as the Divine Spirit.

If you are reading this now, then you are ready to grow towards your greatness. If this book speaks to a truth inside of you, then you are ready to find ways to work spiritually.

PART I

PATH FOR GREATNESS

1

WORK AS SPIRITUAL SERVICE

*I am only one; but still I am one. I cannot do everything, but
still I can do something; I will not refuse to do the something I
can do.*

– Helen Keller

Our path to greatness comes when we see our life as an
opportunity to serve. Since we spend most of our
waking hours at work, it is important to see how we can
spiritually serve others in our work. Appreciating the efforts
of a co-worker or providing her encouragement may be just
what she needs to handle the stress in her life. The ripple
effect of a kind deed extends beyond what we realize. When
work is seen as a way to serve others with love, we help
ourselves and others grow towards spiritual greatness. We
nourish the soul. This book is about growing spiritually at
work. It is about offering loving service at work through the
daily, seemingly insignificant interactions with others. When
we look for the limitless opportunities we have to serve others,

we see how each day brings more chances to follow our path of spiritual greatness and help others grow towards their greatness.

The metaphor of a flower may be used to illustrate spiritual greatness.

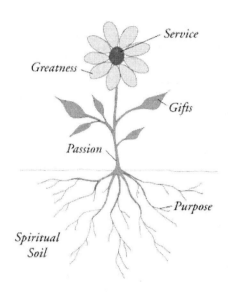

We all need spiritually fertile soil from which to grow. Our spiritual values and principles provide us with the essential elements we need to thrive. Our purpose is the roots that firmly ground us in the world and provide sustenance for our work. Our passion stems from our purpose. Our passion holds us up, as the stem of a flower, and extends us to new heights. A person lacking passion shows no vigor for life, has no energy to carry their load, just as a flower lays limp and wilted without a strong stem.

Our gifts allow us to offer our service to others. Just as a leaf draws in light to make new energy for the plant, our gifts bring life to our work as service. Our authentic self and our unique attributes support our essence as a spiritual being to be of spiritual service to others. The center of the flower is service; our offering to the world is the sweet nectar contained in that flower. Others draw food and sustenance from the service we provide. Finally, to complete the metaphor, the petals of the flower are the brilliance we bring forth in our lives. Our greatness shines in the beauty of who we are as unique spiritual people.

Thus, personal spiritual greatness comes from having fertile soil (spiritual inspiration, values, and principles), firm roots (purpose), strong stem (passion), developed leaves (gifts), and sweet nectar (service). Your greatness of character, your authenticity, and your integrity blossom out in the magnificence of your being.

CULTIVATING YOUR SPIRITUAL VALUES AND PRINCIPLES

We must be intentional about cultivating our spiritual soil. Rich fertile soil provides us the nourishment to blossom rather than to wither and never reach our fullest potential. At times the complexity of life seems to overwhelm us and our spiritual groundedness seems shaky. It is tempting to take the path of least resistance, become apathetic and give up, or to look out only for ourselves. However, life's reward comes in being a part of the greater dance. The path for greatness starts by answering the challenges before us with courage and conviction. The path for greatness beckons us to choose to live authentically, morally, true to our divine spirit.

Our actions are grounded in our spiritual values and sustained by continual spiritual inspiration. We must keep our spiritual soil nourished by finding sources of inspiration. Because the soil is porous, be open to the multitude of ways you can replenish your spiritual nutrients. It is important to take time to cultivate your spiritual soil, for it is what will sustain you throughout your life and nourish you in difficult times.

A necessary first step in cultivating your spiritual values and principles is to be clear on those lessons that instruct you and guide you to greater spiritual growth. There are several ways to do this. Review books that were instrumental in teaching you how to live spiritually or have been sources of inspiration. Several of the books referenced in the bibliography can help you with this.

Identify those personal qualities that you want to cultivate and renew in your life. Throughout this book, I will refer to spiritual values and principles that seem universal such as compassion, forgiveness, integrity, interdependence, and authenticity. Compile a list of what spirituality means to you. Brainstorm words that describe what a spiritual life is like. Look through a book on values clarification.

Post the set of values and principles you believe are worth living by; be sure they are somewhere visible so you can refer to them regularly. Engage in activities that help you reflect on and examine them. Bring these values and principles to your awareness through daily meditation or prayer. Put those principles on paper and keep them in your wallet, review them periodically, and ask yourself how you are living them at that moment. Make them a real part of your life.

One short affirmation you can say in the morning over breakfast or in the shower is "Today I will offer more _____ (state the value) than I did yesterday." Then in the evening take stock of your day to see how you lived out that value or

12

principle. Daily reflection on how we live our lives in accordance with our values is an important part of cultivating our spiritual soil.

Stories of Greatness

Stories shed light on difficult problems and offer hopeful solutions and inspiration for meeting our challenges. The success of the *Chicken Soup for the Soul* book series speaks to the yearning we have for stories to sustain our lives. Throughout this book, examples are presented of people and organizations that exemplify characteristics of greatness. Here are some examples of people who show the breadth of ways greatness comes by serving others.

Sharing Her Gifts

Growing up in a poor working class family, Melissa Bradley's dream was to make a million dollars by the time she was 30. When she accomplished that dream by age 26 she realized there was more to life than money. Life for Melissa involved improving others' lives. Indeed, her personal mission statement is about changing the paradigms of capitalism so that people of color are not oppressed.

Though she was a bright student, as an African American in a predominately white high school, Melissa's guidance counselors didn't encourage her to attend college. Many of her friends were either taking local minimum wage jobs, joining the military, or not finishing school. She wanted to attend college because she felt that it was her ticket to becoming a millionaire.

Melissa graduated from Georgetown University in 1989 with a degree in finance and worked for a year with Sallie Mae, a student loan agency, as a Marketing and Finance Specialist. Though her first year performance review was positive, she was told that she wouldn't be promoted unless someone died or retired. Shortly afterwards she started plans for her own business as a financial investment advisor. She did her homework, developed a business plan, and went to the Small Business Administration to get a small loan to start her company. The loan officer liked the plan but said Melissa had three strikes against her. She was young (23 years old), black, and female, all attributes that (according to conventional wisdom) worked against being a financial investment advisor.

Although frustrated that her expensive college degree didn't get her where she wanted to be, she wasn't discouraged. Melissa Bradley is a woman who isn't stopped by walls. She knew there wasn't anything that could be done about who she was, so she used the severance pay from her previous job, borrowed a few hundred dollars from her mother, and hustled. Working out of an office in her apartment, Melissa provided the financial advising she knew best, getting students through college. She networked with PTA members and neighborhood parents to build up her business. She formed a business partnership with another woman to provide out-placement services to companies that were downsizing. Melissa offered financial advising for how to invest severance pay, while her business partner offered the psychological services necessary for finding other work. Three years later, at age 26, she sold the company for over a million dollars.

Her path for greatness didn't end with being a millionaire by age 30. She was born to do more than that. During both the time she attended college and the time she built her first company, Melissa performed volunteer work with juvenile delinquents. She quickly discovered that these kids were not likely to ever get a job that paid more than minimum wage due to their criminal records. She knew about being an entrepreneur; the youth with whom she worked wanted to be business owners. She started a program with some friends that taught these teens business skills. Most of these kids already had the qualities of entrepreneurs; they just didn't know how to use their gifts and passion constructively.

Melissa founded The Entrepreneurial Development Institute (TEDI), which seeks to empower disadvantaged youth to develop small businesses, avoid drugs and crime, and sharpen academic skills. She worked with the youth from 8:00 am to 1:00 am – before school, after school, or during midnight basketball.

After Melissa sold her first company, she set up a loan program using her personal funds for several youth who went through her training to start their own business. Since no bank would give teenagers the start-up capital they needed, Melissa became the banker. She offered $1,500 loans to teens who had their business plans in place so they could get their businesses off the ground. The program was so successful it received recognition from the mayor of Washington D.C. and several foundations. Two of the youth developed and later sold a board game to Parker Brothers for a sizable amount of money, and another youth started a catering business.

This program not only helped troubled teens develop important business skills and taught them how to start and run a business, but the youth were so excited about it they started getting their lives in order. The dropout rates, truancy rates, and recidivism rates of the teens who completed the program fell significantly. After three years of working for TEDI, she saw another need for these youth, and so resigned her position.

Bank regulations are intentionally rigid about making loans that are too risky in order to protect investors in banks. Thus, most of the teens in the TEDI program wouldn't be eligible for capital funds to grow their company. Melissa started a venture capital firm at age 31 to provide financial resources to those people usually left out of the bank lending system, namely minorities and women. These populations typically don't have the credit and/or have too large a debt load to get funding from banks.

Melissa wants to prove to large investment firms that they can be profitable by supporting these minority or "risky" enterprises. She is a woman not only of high energy and passion, but enormous integrity and soul. Her purpose is clear, her gifts are polished, and her greatness is evident to anyone privileged to meet her.

TROUBADOUR OF GREATNESS

One of my personal heroes is Bill Breeden. I had the privilege of getting to know Bill when I was a graduate student in Bloomington, Indiana in the 1980s. Bill was living with his family on a farm outside of town. Several years before I met Bill, I read in our local paper that he had served for one season as Director of Migrant Ministry for the Indiana Council of Churches. In this role he helped migrant farm workers get adequate water and sewer systems in the camps where they lived on Indiana farms. I would never have known there were such farms in Indiana had Bill not been a witness to the inhospitable conditions.

At first glance, Bill is not someone who would strike you as being remarkable. To see him in his worn jeans and work shirt, you might think he is a typical blue-collar worker living a simple life. He has worked most of his life earning little money. But money is clearly not his motivation for working on the projects he does.

Bill is one of the finest examples of spiritual groundedness for personal greatness I know. He grew up in the Nazarene Church and went to seminary to become a minister. After six years of serving Disciples of Christ churches, he realized that being a parish minister was not the way for him to fully live his faith. He wanted to be a full-time parent to his two children. Eventually he moved his family to Spencer, Indiana where he took various jobs, from truck driving to teaching criminal justice at Indiana University. Bill also has preached at various Unitarian Universalist churches in the area.

Bill is a troubadour for justice, and his deep faith and conviction have led him to some remarkable experiences. He has been arrested on several occasions for acting on his faith. I met Bill when I was working on efforts to stop the civil war in El Salvador. I was doing my small part to educate people about the US foreign policy that fed the death and destruction in Central America. During the time I got to know Bill, he was working to make a direct impact and improve the human condition. One remarkable story about Bill's unwavering faith came when he agreed to lead a caravan to bring medical and humanitarian aid to the people in Polsetega, Nicaragua (a sister city of Bloomington). The year was 1989, the illegal U.S.-funded Contra war was in its final stages, and civil wars raged in Guatemala, Honduras, and El Salvador.

We must have the courge to enter the belly of the beast and look squarely at the problems of our day.

— Bill Breeden

In a talk Bill gave to our church on his return from that trip, he spoke of the courage needed to "enter the belly of the beast." Bill's courage and conviction is a light that has guided my work on many occasions. Bill challenged us to look squarely at the problems of the day and seek to remedy them.

Bill told how he talked his way past a border patrol (they thought the truck he was driving would be used for military purposes). When he was later stopped by a Honduran military patrol, his courage and conviction were tested. He was about to be searched by military men when he remembered he had a letter in his pocket to his wife describing the events on the trip. He feared the letter would be used against him if turned over to hostile military personnel. In the urgency of the moment, he knew the only way to get rid of the evidence while the men were searching his truck was to eat it! Bill and two friends were handcuffed, blindfolded, and hauled in the back of a truck to a military prison in the mountains. There were detained and interrogated for three and a half days before being released.

In 1998, Bill agreed to return to Nicaragua with a truckload of aid for victims of Hurricane Mitch. Within three weeks of the storm, the Pastors for Peace caravan, of which his truck was a part, rolled into Nicaragua.

He stands tall among those who walk the talk. By his example, he spreads the message that our lives are meant to serve others. He has the courage, spiritual guidance, and faith to do his work in the face of enormous adversity. His passion and gifts help him serve others. His gifts of oration and song are particularly moving. I look forward to hearing about Bill's next project because I know I will be inspired to do better in my corner of the world. Bill helps me see that we all have a larger role to play as change agents for a better world.

TABLE FOR 6 BILLION PLEASE

Judy Wicks is the founder and proprietor of the White Dog Cafe in Philadelphia. She says she "uses good food to lure people in for social activism." Her food is quite a lure. What started as a simple cafe, literally in her apartment living room with a grill in the backyard, has now grown into a cafe that takes up four buildings, with a staff of 100 people. In 1998, gross receipts for the White Dog Cafe were over $4 million. In an adjacent building, she has opened a shop for purchasing goods made by indigenous people around the globe.

Judy believes in buying products directly from places that need U.S. support for their local economy. She travels to countries to speak to the food growers to set up special purchasing agreements. She makes a point to get to know the people who will be supplying the food for her customers. Judy set up an international sister restaurant program called "Table for 6 Billion Please" as her way to help feed the world. She started her business with an interest in not just feeding those of us in the land of plenty.

Judy looks for ways to establish business contacts with people regardless of whether our country sees them as friends. Judy refers to this as "eating with the enemy." She wants to "bake bread together to create world peace." She firmly believes that if we are to build a more just society and attain world peace, we must establish direct connections with people and find ways to work with them so that they can benefit directly.

Judy is a leader in two important business associations (Business for Social Responsibility and the Social Venture Network) that encourage businesses to incorporate social responsibility into their business culture and operations. Judy has a strong sense of social justice that is integral to her business. This includes a steadfast belief that businesses are capable of operating in a way that leaves the world enriched and not scarred. Her unique approach to entrepreneurship and corporate social responsibility has been highlighted in a Harvard Business School case and video.

In her work with the Social Venture Network, she sees the integration of entrepreneurship, social activism, and spirituality leading to a more just world, with greater personal development also taking place.

Boulders along the Spiritual Path

My husband and I had been struggling over where to live to accommodate the distance between his work and mine for well over a year. We finally found a situation that seemed to work perfectly for us. One evening, as we negotiated a contract on a house, we got into a major fight. We were so close to resolution on the house, yet we couldn't seem to reach closure on it. I reluctantly agreed to the price he wanted to offer, but I didn't feel good about the way that we handled ourselves in getting to the decision.

I didn't sleep well that night and was still fuming the next day. I felt he didn't understand the underlying issues that I was raising (having little to do with the house at that point). I also knew I had not been very caring or respectful, let alone compassionate or understanding, in dealing with him. I let his fears trigger my own baggage about power and control in our relationship. I couldn't get the fight off my mind; I kept going over what we said and what didn't get said. It just kept nagging at me.

While I had done a little better during the fight than normal (I took a time out to breathe and meditate on what was going on), I still didn't handle the situation in a loving, compassionate way. This was particularly disturbing since the crux of the fight (at least my side of the fight) was how we were going to be more supportive of each other. The fight was dripping with irony.

As I was driving to pick up the contract at the realtor's office, I had a flash of insight. I realized this fight was just the experience I needed to practice being more compassionate and understanding when I was angry. I had obviously failed this exercise. Then it dawned on me that I would continue to feel lousy about arguments with him or others until I got the lesson right. I about lost my breath at this point. The thought of going through too many more fights like that one scared me.

After a minute of stunned silence at the enormity of this insight, I began to laugh. It felt so good to laugh too. I needed to stretch my face muscles, which had been tight the past fifteen hours. I needed a good belly laugh to relax my abdomen that also was feeling twisted and tight. I laughed from deep within because I could see so clearly how that fight was just what I needed. It was a gift from God. I needed to see how I fought in stressful times and how to adjust during them. I needed to see the lessons involved and to know that I could change course to be more compassionate even in my anger.

> *At funerals people don't talk about growth rates. They talk about love, generosity, and trust.*
> — Tom Chappell, CEO Tom's of Maine

The argument we had was merely a drama being acted out. Unfortunately, in this situation I didn't see the drama for the offering that it was — to be spiritually grounded and open to greater understanding. The key for us to live spiritually with others, especially in conflict situations, is to see the drama for what it is *while being in the middle of it*. Once that awareness becomes clear, we can choose to shift gears, to change the script to one of greater loving kindness.

The path for greatness rarely is an easy path to follow. It will take many steps, and many more missteps, to get it right. But the point of this book, indeed I believe the point of life, is to see the path we are on more clearly, to learn along the way, and to do better on each new hill we climb.

We each touch the lives of so many. All of us have a choice to make in how we write the story of our lives. The path for greatness means making the choice to fulfill a higher purpose with our lives and to embody our highest ideals.

2

FINDING YOUR PURPOSE
IN VOCATION

*Becoming faithful to our gifts and inclinations, hearing the call
or press within to be whole, we find vocation— that line of
activity we intentionally use to grow as a person.*

— Marsha Sinetar, *To Build the Life You Want,
Create the Work You Love*

I remember a married couple that had constant disagreements because of their different views of work. The husband grew up believing that you "live to work" and the wife grew up believing that you "work to live." These two views of work underlie the notion of work as an activity *separate from life* rather than as an integral part of life. Both views have major ramifications on how much time, energy, and emotional investment one has in one's work. To the wife, a job was meant to provide the resources to do other things in life revolving around family, church, or community. To the husband it was important to find a job that was interesting and challenging and was an outlet for his talents. Needless to say, they had many disagreements about how much time they should spend at their jobs.

This difference is more than just a matter of time allocation. There is a danger of going too far in the extreme of either position. If one only "works to live," then any job that provides the resources to meet other interests will do. The implications for work motivation is clear. According to this view, work motivation will be sustained only so long as the paycheck and security are guaranteed. In addition, when one's lifestyle changes the paycheck will need to reflect the new (and usually more expensive) lifestyle. People

Life and livelihood ought not be separate, but to flow from the same source, which is Spirit.

— Matthew Fox

who subscribe to this view will feel fairly anxious in this day of downsizing and corporate restructuring. If work holds no other role other than to provide a paycheck, it has little connection with self.

People subscribing to the "'live to work" philosophy run the risk of workaholism. Addiction to work causes damage not only to the worker and his family, but creates unhealthy organizations as well. Workaholics aren't able to balance their lives to make room for other activities that make them whole. They often use work to hide from personal problems. Workaholics use work as an escape mechanism to avoid facing difficult life circumstances, such as unhealthy relationships or personal, emotional pain. Instead, we should heed the words of Matthew Fox, "Life and livelihood ought not be separate, but to flow from the same source, which is Spirit."

RIGHT LIVELIHOOD

Because people spend so much of their waking life in work, The Buddha recognized that Right Livelihood is a vehicle to practice morality in work and find Enlightenment. Right Livelihood is work that does no harm and brings people closer to Ultimate Wisdom. Right Livelihood[1] is the fifth step along the Buddhist Eightfold Path to Enlightenment. Through Right Livelihood one can practice Right Understanding, Right Thought, Right Speech, and Right Action.

The focus of Right Livelihood is not on having a particular job or doing a specific type of work, but on the process and way of being through one's work. Right Livelihood is joyful and serves others. It helps us grow and learn; it fits who we are. Through Right Livelihood, we see work being as much a vacation as a vocation. Most importantly, Right Livelihood helps us see how we are all part of the Web of Life, and thus does not entail bringing harm to others, society, or the earth.

Right Livelihood is a creative process, ever-unfolding and ever-changing. As we learn and grow, our Right Livelihood must change to allow us to grow and use more of our gifts. We must continually examine who we are and what we need to do to fulfill our purpose. We will use and develop different gifts at different stages of our lives.

VOCATION AS A CALLING

Our challenge is to find or create opportunities that allow us to work from our Source of energy and love. Some people may need to search deeply to find that Source. However, which path you follow is not as important as *how* you follow that path. Marsha Sinetar, author of several books on finding wholeness and happiness through work, describes vocation as "our deepest summons to be human in a particular way." In her book *To Build the Life You Want, Create the Work You Love*, Sinetar notes, "optimal life requires meaningful vocation — some active, contributive, relational work to help us become unique whole persons. Until we achieve this integration, we live but half a life."

Like Jonah, you may seek other adventures, only to be swallowed up by experiences larger than yourself, and finally to be spit out so that you can pursue your true purpose. It is like Abraham saying to God, "Here I am."

— Bill Breeden

This integration is referred to as "finding your calling" because it is a spiritual pursuit. Finding your calling requires understanding the entirety of who you are and doesn't happen at the exclusion of other parts of your life. Your calling must serve the wholeness of your being. It requires you to believe you have something to offer others.

Most people are familiar with clergy that feel "called" to the ministry. For these people, the calling comes from a deep place within them that directs them to serve God in a particular way. Likewise, many teachers speak of a calling to educate children. A calling comes from a deep passion to serve in some manner; it is more than a career or occupation. Having a calling means finding work that is an outlet for your unique talents and that fulfills a deep sense of purpose for your life. Your calling is something that you may run from but it is always within you. Authentic vocation is an expression of your soul. Like Jonah, you may seek other adventures, only to be swallowed up by experiences larger than yourself, and finally to be spit out so that you can pursue your true purpose.[2] It is like Abraham saying to God, "Here I am." We are all called to serve a life purpose, and by doing so, we become whole, authentic people.

Some people are fortunate to know from a very young age what it is they "want to do when they grow up." They have an inner direction that compels them to pursue life experiences and find opportunities that will help them fulfill their life mission. My brother knew from the age of 10 that he wanted to be an architect. This sense of calling kept him going through numerous all-night studio work in college and intense job searching during economic downturns. Today, he is a successful architect managing several multimillion dollar projects.

He shared a story of a memorable Halloween night when he was in college. He and some friends were putting in an all-nighter to complete a project and could hear music from nearby apartments and fraternity parties. Around 2 a.m. one student threw down her pencil and said, "Why are we in here slaving away when everyone else is having a good time?" After a very long difficult silence, my brother said, "Because I never imagined myself being anything else besides an architect." Without exception, everyone in that room conveyed the same sentiments. For the next 20 minutes they stopped their work to tell how they had known from a young age they wanted to be architects. When they finished their stories, they continued working through the night not complaining that they were missing the parties.

Those who have known all their life what they wanted to do have a deep sense of what they are meant to do. These people are fortunate to have that clarity and determination to fully live out their life mission. I have a childhood friend who, for as long as I can remember, wanted to be a doctor. We attended the same college, and on the eve of her taking the medical entrance exam, I stopped by Jenny's house to bring her some flowers and wish her luck. She said "Most of my friends here don't understand why I push myself so hard and study so much. But it means a lot to me that you do." Later at her medical school graduation, I felt such joy knowing Jenny had achieved all that she had wanted for so many years.

Both of these stories are examples of people who have a deep knowing of who they are and what they are called to do. For many others this calling may take decades. It is even likely that one's calling will change several times over the course of a lifetime as interests and life circumstances change. A former colleague said her life mission in her 20s and 30s was to raise her children to be healthy and well-adjusted people. She chose to stay home and not pursue a career to focus her energy on her calling as a parent. After her children went off to college she pursued another calling. She was able to build a career on her past volunteer experiences and community involvement working with nonprofit organizations. Though my colleague was intimidated at first going into the job market after being out of it for over twenty years, she knew what her skills were and that she could put them to good use. She also knew that her career venture would need to serve the wholeness of her being.

God will not ask me why I was not Moses. He will ask me why I was not Susyah.
– Hasidic Rabbi Susyah

Although one's calling to serve may change as life circumstances change, what is critical is how we answer the call. The calling to use our gifts uniquely is a prompting of the Spirit that cannot be resisted. If we don't respond to our calling, we risk losing touch with that part of ourselves that makes us whole. As the 18th century Hasidic Rabbi Susyah said, "God will not ask me why I was not Moses. He will ask me why I was not Susyah."

How can you go about finding your calling? It takes careful discernment of who you are and what you have to offer to the world. Many people turn to career counselors or related books to help them discover their skills and interests. Richard Bolles' books on career development have helped countless people find the bigger picture for their lives. As a former minister, Bolles understands the deep connection that work and life have with living fully and authentically.

Activities such as journaling, drawing, meditation, or prayer help to remove the layers of mental chatter so that we can find our own answers. These types of activities must be done regularly and for a sustained period of time to reveal our inner truths and to understand our life mission. Reflecting on our motives and questioning basic assumptions about our lives are important steps in living authentically and with integrity. Other questions to consider in determining your calling:

1. What part of you do you bring forth in your work? Is your work speaking to the wholeness of who you are?

2. Are your gifts and talents currently being used wisely, fully, effectively? If not, how could you draw upon your talents more as an offering to others?

3. Think of moments when you recognized you were being authentic. What conditions allow you to be authentic?

Another activity to bring your life into focus is to write your epitaph or a eulogy that would be read at your memorial service. Once you do this, be intentional about living your life so that it is true.

DISCOVERING MY HIGHER PURPOSE

I began thinking of my vocation as a calling when I felt an unsettled stirring deep within. I realized I needed to bridge my personal spiritual journey with the professional work I did.

I seriously considered the ministry for several years, but felt that serving a church wasn't right for me. I knew I had to combine my training and experience somehow with my spirituality to be my authentic self. Holding both a Masters in psychology and Ph.D. in management, I felt I needed to bridge spirituality and business, though for the longest time I didn't know exactly how that would happen. During the late 1980s and early 1990s, practically no one was talking about spirituality in the workplace. Businesses were only just beginning to take seriously the notion of corporate social responsibility. Having a recycling program at work or an Employee Assistance Program was seen as a progressive thing to do then!

Through the 1990s I was intentional about discovering my calling. I took several jobs that helped me in that journey. I also turned down two jobs that seemed good for external reasons (good pay and high status). I sensed these job opportunities were not the right path for me, not my real calling, even though I wasn't exactly sure what that calling was at the time. It was hard to defend turning down each job, but I knew deep inside they weren't right for me. I sensed they weren't putting me in the direction I needed to go.

At times, what I felt was right for me wasn't what my family thought I "should" do. Out of genuine concern, my mother projected her angst on to me by questioning my ability to follow a different path. It was difficult to trust my inner knowing and pay less attention to "authority people" in my life. But I focused on my faith and the spiritual growth I was going through. I sought greater clarity by practicing meditation and attending workshops related to personal spiritual development. My faith had developed so much during this time that I knew I would be guided to find my highest purpose. And on so many occasions when I needed it, I received affirmations about what was right for me.

In 1994 my husband and I packed all our possessions in storage and traveled for six months to Australia, Asia, Europe, and Israel before we moved to a new town. We hoped for an epiphany during the trip about our next vocational path, but we only grasped vague notions. This trip was truly a leap of faith for us since we didn't have jobs waiting for us when we returned. Yet the time was valuable for our learning and provided a space for clarity to seep through.

When we resettled, I made a conscious effort to discern my higher purpose. Over the next two years, I became more focused on what I wanted to do with my life and wrote a personal mission statement. Based on my personal mission statement, I wrote a professional mission statement which included the following:

To help people find and live their wholeness by:

1. facilitating personal spiritual development,

2. creating and developing environments (e.g., work and community) that are supportive of individual expression and personal growth.

As I started to write this book and give workshops on working spiritually, I knew this type of work was my calling. I draw my passion from it and have the gifts to do it well. I know my vocation serves a Higher Purpose. I am here to help others similarly struggling to find spiritual integration of work and self.

In the process of finding my calling, I contacted two former colleagues who are both doing work related to mine and are very committed to their spiritual journeys. We all felt that we wanted to do something to bring spirituality into the workplace. One outgrowth of a retreat with them was the idea to write this book. Through more time and discernment, I've found that my purpose is to help others work spiritually, either through my college teaching or as a consultant. Over the past five years, I have gathered similarly spiritually inclined teachers and facilitators. We decided to form the WestWind Institute, a training organization that conducts workshops and retreats to help people learn how to bring spirituality to their workplace and how to work spiritually.

This has been my journey – a scary one at times for sure. Yet it is incredibly fulfilling to see others discover more of their wholeness as a result of some activity I've led. You all have unique stories of journeys to discover your calling. If you haven't found your calling, at least take seriously the notion that you have one. Then set out to discover what it is. If your spirit yearns to soar and be heard, answer the call.

If your spirit yearns to soar and be heard, answer the call.

ENTER THE DARKNESS

Finding your calling is not always a pleasant experience. Sometimes it is precipitated by a loss or turbulent period. Often people feel a sense of restlessness or dissatisfaction with what they are doing and feel a sense that there is something else that must be done. Ralph Waldo Emerson calls this period of discomfort "Divine Discontent." Such discontent, while uncomfortable, can be a powerful motivator for people to explore themselves at a deeper level. Later, in chapter 14, I will expand more on the process of facing our fears.

In various mystical traditions, such as in the Shamanic journey, a final stage to wholeness is the process of death and rebirth. Entering into your darkness and facing your fears is often necessary to finding strength and inner resources you didn't know you had. Many people who have reached peak performance have experienced the valleys as well. A common

Buddhist notion is that we can't fill ourselves up unless we are willing to empty ourselves. This emptying process usually involves letting go of old behavior patterns or aspects of our lifestyle to which we cling.

One colleague described an intense period of his life where his job no longer held meaning for him. He experienced a prolonged period of emptiness before he found renewal. He had been a successful salesperson with all the material successes expected for a man of his position. During a flood one year he volunteered through his church to fill sandbags at a levee outside of town. Working next to his crew was a group of convicts also trying to beat the rushing waters. He watched the men work and something came over him, a deep emptiness that he couldn't put his finger on. Over the coming months he realized his house and boat really didn't matter all that much. What mattered was the human condition. Eventually he quit his job, moved, and took another job as the marketing director for a major metropolitan food bank. It was through this work that he later decided to start a lunch cafe for the homeless, and eventually added a drug rehabilitation center to the cafe. He hadn't set out to do such work. However he felt a discontent with his earlier, comfortable life, which emerged from deep within himself. He knew he wouldn't be whole unless he addressed this discontent.

To find your calling you must peel off layers of yourself to hear the still, small voice within.

Making the decision to change careers or shift lifestyles is often difficult. It is best done with support of family and friends. But those who find their calling make such changes even when the changes are met with skepticism or concern. You will recognize that a life change is consistent with your deeper knowing when you can't imagine *not* making the change or pursuing a particular life path.

To find your calling you must peel off layers of yourself to hear the still, small voice within. In this way, you will be authentic. Living authentically and with integrity means knowing yourself well enough that you do what is right for you, not necessarily what others or society feels you *should* do. It means carefully examining all the external messages you were given as a child or learned as an adult to determine what ideas and directions ring true for you.

It is important to sift through the soil of your spiritual values to discern your life purpose. Seek out ways to live those values in your work or find work that allows you

My life is my message.

– Mohandas K. Gandhi

to be true to your life purpose. When you do so, you will gain more energy and passion to share your gifts with others.

EXERCISES

1. Think back over your life and those people and events that shaped you into the person you are today. Lay a piece of paper horizontally and draw a line from left to right, with room to write above and below the line. This is your timeline, starting with your birth and going to your projected time of death.

    a. Indicate on this timeline any major life events and decisions that have occurred until the present. Writing above the line, describe what those events were. Writing below the line, describe what lessons you feel you learned from those experiences. Reflect on how decisions and events shaped your life and/or career today. What patterns emerge?

    b. Projecting into the future, mark those events you hope or expect will happen still in your life. Describe what these events are above the timeline and below the line write what lessons you think you will learn from them.

    c. Are there any changes that you need to make to fulfill your life's passion or purpose? What will help prepare you for those changes?

2. Develop a personal mission statement that expresses what you believe your life purpose is. Keep it to no more than a few sentences; the shorter and clearer the better. How does your work currently fit your life aspirations and life purpose? Craft a professional mission statement consistent with your personal mission statement.

3. What areas of your life would be more fulfilled if your work was your spiritual calling?

For other resources on this topic, refer to these books:

Bolles, Richard N., *What Color is Your Parachute: A Practical Manual for Job-Hunters and Career Changes*, Ten Speed Press, Berkeley, CA, current edition.

Cameron, Julia, *The Artist's Way*, Putnam Publishing, NY, 1995.

Hagan, Kay Leigh, *Prayers to the Moon: Exercises in Self Reflection*, Harper Collins, San Francisco, 1991.

3

USING YOUR GIFTS: SHARING YOUR PASSION

What is the call of your soul? All of us are called to share with the world.

— Rev. Tom Chulak

What is vitally important in fulfilling your life purpose is to recognize and honor your gifts and not "hide them under a bushel." Your inner light can flourish when you believe you have something to offer the world *and* that it is valid for you to offer it to the world. This involves believing in yourself enough to know you have an inner light. Then you must have enough courage to send out your light so that others may see it.

You must continually affirm that you have something unique to offer the world and have the courage to use your gifts. Your gifts may be big and bold, or they may seem fairly trivial. There are an infinite number of ways we can use our gifts to create a better world. Using your gifts to serve others and sharing your passion are essential steps for greatness.

Let's not confuse greatness with ego status. The greatness to which I am referring comes from a greatness of character. Using your gifts to manipulate others for your own gain diminishes your character. Some charismatic leaders have propelled themselves to greatness only to fall just as hard when they misuse their power and influence. You must use your gifts freely *and* wisely to be truly great.

> *I invite you to experience the magnificence of who you are.*
>
> — Jeffrey Swartz

Tom Chappell, Chief Executive Officer (CEO) of Tom's of Maine, urges CEOs to begin their day with humility. He says "we're part of, but not the center of life." Tom and his wife Kate have built their business on the notion that employees want to share their gifts. Tom believes, "When given an opportunity for goodness, it's hard to turn it down."

ENTREPRENEURS AND ARTISTS USE THEIR GIFTS

Many of today's entrepreneurs, particularly women, start from a desire to integrate all parts of themselves with their work. Often people will venture out on their own because they feel they can best use their talents in jobs they create. They start their own business as a way to use their gifts fully. Other entrepreneurs start a business out of a negative impulse from their previous work, especially if it was an environment in which they were stifled mentally or spiritually. It is important to know what you are moving *from*, as well as to know what you are *creating*.

Most entrepreneurs endure long hours of work to build their businesses. Consequently, they won't be successful unless they feel passion for their work. Though most small businesses fail because they don't have enough capital, the human capital of energy and talent must also be there. You must offer your unique gifts and have plenty of passion to follow the difficult path of being an entrepreneur. Entrepreneurs who work from rich spiritual soil use their gifts based on their calling. They rejuvenate their passion by nurturing their spirituality. Indeed, to be an entrepreneur is an act of faith. "Creating something that has never existed is a faith-based assertion," according to Jeffrey Swartz, CEO of Timberland Company.

If you are considering venturing out on you own, be sure to examine your motives for such a move. Do you want to be in business to make money, or do you want to make money to stay in business? How you answer that question shows what motivations and aspirations you have for your work. If your intention and purpose are to offer the best of who you are to the world, money becomes merely a flow of energy to allow your gifts to come forth. Your business, sustained by money and other energy sources, becomes the vehicle by which you will be of service to the world.

If you want to create your own business or start a new venture, talk to others who have done so. In this way, you will have a realistic idea of what is involved. You must be willing to make personal sacrifices to create your dreams. Most importantly, you will need the passion to sustain you in the difficult moments. You will need to love what you are doing so that you can stay committed, even when you are frustrated and want to walk away.

Many artists, like entrepreneurs, have a deep passion to use their gifts. Some take routine jobs so they can focus on their art, while others find positions that allow them to use their gifts in their work. A friend of mine wanted to play the trumpet again after many years of not playing. He took a part time job so that he had time to practice and get his mouth back in condition for performance level playing. After some months he tried out for a community orchestra and was accepted. However, with time he didn't find it as rewarding as he had hoped. Rather than feel discouraged by the experience he went deeper into his longing to play music. After several months of uncertainty, he began playing the piano, which he also had learned earlier. I met him in the process of rediscovering his love of music as a singular passion in his life. He described his desire to practice as almost an obsession. He said, "It was as if God was grabbing me by the shoulders and putting me in front of a piano saying 'You were born to play this'."

Our need to be creative is powerful. I recently saw an art show and was struck by one piece by a Ukranian sculptor, Alexandr Reut. Next to his work was this quote: "I know that I have talent, but that it does not belong to me. I am just in temporary possession of it. One day, God, who really owns it, will ask me, "What did I do? Did I waste my time or did I put the gift He gave me to good use?"

Even if you are not an entrepreneur or artist, think of your work as an activity that calls forth the fullness of your being. Work as a spiritual activity goes beyond merely having a job to fill the space of your life. It allows you to find meaning in what you do, to fulfill your higher purpose, to let your light shine before all. Work must be rooted in your purpose. It must use your gifts, stem from your passion, and flower into service.

SHARING YOUR PASSION

Those people who reach their potential serving others know how to share their gifts and use their passion effectively. I'm not talking about workaholism, where you lose perspective of your role in your world. It is just the opposite. The path for greatness includes being ever mindful of who you are, how you serve, and what kind of relationships you have with others. Charismatic people often have this kind of passion; they inspire us to be better than we currently are. They spend time giving to the world and take time to replenish their reserves.

If you've ever been around someone passionate about what they do you know how infectious it can be. Sometimes the passion comes from a simple but profound experience. Jeffrey Swartz described his first experience at doing corporate community service work. He was chief operating officer (COO) of Timberland at the time and had given some Timberland boots to a youth serving organization called City Year. The head of City Year came to Swartz's office afterwards and asked Jeffrey if he wanted to "experience the magnificence of your being." Though unsure what it would lead to, Jeffrey took up the call.

Swartz agreed to paint a local drug and alcohol rehabilitation center. He worked alongside a teen who was in the rehab program. The teen asked Swartz what he did, and Jeffrey tried to answer as simply as he could what a COO of a company does. Then to keep the teen engaged in the conversation, Swartz asked the teen what he did. The teen replied, "I don't *do* anything, I try to *be* well." That teenager taught Jeffrey the difference between doing and being. It left such a strong impression on Swartz, he now encourages other corporate leaders to do community service work, not just for the community, but for their personal growth.

Think of a time when you felt truly inspired. Did you feel more passionate about life as a result? How did you share your enthusiasm or passion with others? How did you sustain your passion? I was recently told that the word "enthusiasm" comes from the Greek phrase "en-theos" meaning "in God." Thus, when we work with enthusiasm we are working in God's presence. Our passion is sustained when we connect with that greater spirit working through us.

Look back at all the times you've felt inspired and passionate to act. By extending the roots of your life purpose deeply into your spiritual soil, you'll find ways to sustain your passion and offer your gifts to others. When you have passion and offer your gifts to others, you will be true to the magnificent expression of God that you are.

USING THE GIFT OF COMPASSION

Compassionate understanding is an important ingredient for greatness. It is not, however, something that comes very easily to most of us. We must practice compassionate understanding continually so that it begins to feel more natural. The biggest barrier to compassionate understanding is righteous indignation. We must learn how to offer forgiveness and compassionate understanding even if we feel we are right. If the struggle to prove our righteousness becomes our primary concern, we then lose the bigger picture in the process. When we focus more on who is right than what is right, we venture down an unhealthy and unproductive path.

Compassionate understanding is a gift we give ourselves as well as to others. We often carry enormous stress and tension in our bodies by holding grudges or taking a righteous stance. When we practice compassionate understanding we get rid of the headaches from standing so high on our horses. We begin to see the perspectives of others and perhaps learn something new about ourselves as well.

Offering the other cheek or responding compassionately doesn't mean we need to be silent if there is an injustice or unethical behavior happening. We may need to stand up and be heard so that a perpetrator knows that his action is noted. Gandhi's nonviolence movement was not passive at all, but rather came from the firmness of truth. Speaking out against a wrong action that's directed at you or others is often a difficult spiritual act to perform. The criteria to judge whether or not you are acting spiritually is the intention you have as you speak or take action. If you speak with cruelty, you only add injury to the situation. If you speak with compassion to the person who is causing harm, you raise awareness for that person that her behavior must change, and you offer your understanding and forgiveness. This gives the other person a chance to change without fear of your rejection or retribution.

Most people respond in anger because they feel threatened. The best response for fear is to offer compassionate understanding and encouragement. We can do this when we connect with that place of Divine Love within us and the other. If someone lashes out at you, he may be uncertain or afraid of something. If you ask in an affirming and supportive way what may be troubling him, you not only de-escalate the situation, but you help him understand what is really the underlying issue.

You need to find your center of spiritual groundedness so that you do not get hooked into another person's anger or fear. I find it helpful to take a few deep breaths and say an affirmation such as "May peace enter this situation." Or when you engage with someone who lashes out at you, answer with something like, "I see you are upset. How can you be supported right now?" When you acknowledge the other person's feelings and encourage her to act from her inner strength, she gains confidence in herself as well as feels acceptance and understanding from you. In a work situation, you will need to demonstrate your compassion so that others see they can act another way.

Pema Chödrön is a Buddhist nun who focuses her teaching on compassionate living. In her book, *Start Where You Are*, Chödrön describes a set of Buddhist slogans as part of her teaching to help train the mind. Most of the slogans teach the ever-changing nature of life and how to let go of attachments, whether they are fears or desires. According to lojong practice (mind training) we must rest in the fundamental openness of life. It is too easy to lash out at others who have hurt us. That is why we need to train ourselves to act with compassion when we feel hurt.

We don't have to wait until we are healed to reach out to others. We don't have to wait for someone else to apologize before we can forgive them. We don't have to finish all our personal work before we can be of service to others. In fact, our spiritual growth and inner journey is never completed. We continually learn more ways to be understanding, compassionate, and forgiving. Our life's journey is the practice.

GETTING PAST LEARNED LIMITATIONS

How many things did you want to do or be when you grew up but were told somewhere along the way you couldn't or shouldn't. Messages come in the form of "girls can't do that," "only nerds do that," or "you have to have a job that can support your family." From a very early age, we are taught what we can or cannot do. These messages can be so deeply engrained that we aren't even aware that they influence us. Perhaps only years later, when we have a chance to try something new, do we invoke these messages from deep within our mental storage.

I was interested in juvenile justice work in college but gave up the idea after taking a course in it. My sociology professor said that to really make a difference in the life of juveniles we needed to be a juvenile judge or a lawmaker to enact broad-based changes. The real lesson here is this: *it never occurred to me* that I could be either a judge or a law maker. In part that was because I didn't think women could be judges or lawmakers, but also I didn't believe I had the gifts necessary to excel in these careers. Mentoring programs and programs like "Take Your Daughter To Work" are so important to give young people a chance to see how they can use their gifts and consider various careers that might be available to them.

My sister-in-law recounted a conversation with a co-worker on a summer job during college. The co-worker told Karen she should give up her place in architecture school for a male student. The co-worker believed that because she was a woman, Karen would never be an architect so she shouldn't waste the spot that could be taken by a man. Karen has led a fulfilling and successful career as an architect for the past twenty years.

Similarly, Elizabeth Dole frequently shares her story of her first week at Harvard Law School in the 1960s. An upperclassman told her she should quit school so her spot could go to a male student. This upperclassman told Elizabeth she would never use her law degree so she shouldn't deprive a man from going to school at Harvard. We may think such sentiment is not held today, but unfortunately there are still fields, such as engineering and physics, that young women and minorities are not encouraged to pursue. Luckily for my sister-in-law, Elizabeth Dole, and Melissa Bradley, they believed enough in their purpose and gifts to live their passion.

A friend of mine is very gifted and has many interests he could pursue to work more joyfully. Though he has many talents, he grew up in a household where he experienced constant criticism and fearful world views. As a result, he now has internalized his father's criticism and insecurities. Thus, he feels more comfortable following a conventional career, where he is fairly successful, rather than venture off to explore other career options that use more of his talents and gifts. He is wilting from within because he's too afraid to try other jobs where his other gifts could be used. It may take years to erase these well-learned limiting self-images, but it's vitally important to shed them if we are to use our gifts fully and live with passion and purpose.

Perfectionism is another limiting factor to exploring our gifts. Perfectionism stifles people from expanding their skills into new areas. Perfectionists fear failure or fear learning by trial and error. Most of us have untapped gifts because we aren't willing to take the chance to try our hand at something new. Too many people are afraid to try new things for fear of being inadequate. One story that had a strong impact on me in college is from Leo Buscaglia's book, *Living, Loving and Learning*. This story teaches us to move past our fears or concerns of inadequacy. It illustrates how we grow when we discover and use our gifts to serve others.

Buscaglia shares a story of Joel, a student in one of his classes. Buscaglia had given the class an assignment to go out and do something meaningful for someone else. Joel looked puzzled and asked Buscaglia after class what he should do. Buscaglia told Joel to go find something. After several weeks Joel stopped by after class and again said, "there's nothing to do." Buscaglia drove the student to a nearby nursing home, walked into the sitting room, and motioned across the room with a sweep of his hand saying, "tell me there is nothing to do." Joel looked frightened and asked, "what do I do?" Buscaglia retorted, "go talk to them, sit with them."

Later in the semester, when the assignment was due, Joel bounced up to Buscaglia and said what a valuable experience it had been for him to go to the nursing home. He learned so much from the people he talked to and found such joy in being with them. The days that Joel visited the nursing home became known as "Joel's day." Joel had learned to overcome his fears and found his passion and gifts by doing so.

When sitting just sit. When walking just walk. But above all, don't wobble.

— Buddhist saying

Another story about turning a fearful situation into a positive experience comes from a friend of mine in India. In her home town of Madras there is a businessman who became quite successful, though his earlier lot in life was anything but privileged. He was a poor man from the country who came to the city of Madras to find work. He slept on a train platform every night while he looked for work during the day. One day early in the morning a police officer came walking towards him. The man feared he would be arrested, so he ran away with the police officer in close pursuit.

Near this train platform is the U.S. Embassy. Every day, there were long lines of students or families waiting to get into the Embassy to get a visa to the U.S. The man jumped into the crowds hoping the police officer wouldn't see him. Sure enough the police officer didn't find him.

The poor man started asking why everyone was standing in line. The lines to the embassy stretched for blocks and people would have to wait for days to get inside. As a result, it was not unusual for whole families to camp out while waiting in line, with family members taking turns to get food or drinks. While standing in line, someone tapped the poor man on the shoulder and said he'd pay the poor man a few ruppees to hold this man's place. The poor man eagerly obliged, not really believing he could make money by simply standing in line. The gentleman returned and paid the poor man for his time. As the poor man walked down the line it occurred to him that someone else might want a place held. He managed to spend all day in line getting paid to stand in someone's place.

He spent several weeks making money this way. Then he got the idea to offer to go get drinks or food for people and later he decided to set up a food stand for those in line. He started a business catering to the people standing in line and eventually became a businessman using his ingenuity for other ventures. This businessman is fairly well known in Madras and was written up in the local newspaper. In the article, he thanked Vishnu for his continued protection and thanked the police officer who chased him off the train platform for his good fortune!

Just like the Taoist story of the Chinese farmer who's son tried to tame the wild horses and broke his leg, only to be spared the next year from going to war, you never know whether the barriers or unfortunate experiences are for the best. You must stay open to your life experiences, even if they seem negative at the time. They may simply be the gifts we are given to grow or change in important new ways.

There is a Buddhist saying, "When sitting, just sit. When walking, just walk. But above all, don't wobble." Too often, our passion and purpose are wobbly because we are unsure of what to do with our life experiences. Our gifts may lie dormant, hidden underneath our self doubts and insecurities. However, we may never discover our greatest joy unless we expand our horizons or stretch our comfort levels. Too many people grew up with messages that were critical or judgmental, and thus they learned to doubt themselves. You *can* discover your gifts and find clarity for your purpose in life. When you discover your purpose and use your gifts to the fullest, your walk through life will be strong and sure. You'll have the passion to move forward.

EXERCISES

Write down a story about a time you succeeded at something and/or felt really good about something you accomplished. Don't be bashful about affirming your successes. Explain how and why you were able to succeed.

1. Go through the story and see what personal qualities you had/used/showed in reaching your accomplishment. If you have trouble doing this, share the story with some friends and ask them to reflect on the qualities you had/used/showed.

2. List these qualities. These often form the basis of our unique gifts.

3. What other qualities do you want to nurture and grow so that they also become your gifts?

library
- Focus & concentration & attention to detail.
- Focus on Quality
- creating identity
- organising & structuring
- good communicator
- determination
- passion
+ open for new things, courage
- taking risks

3) - Developing a niche market.
   for library
- developing efficiency

48

4

The Spirituality of Work

When you work you are a flute through whose heart the
whispering of the hours turns to music.

– Kahlil Gibran, *The Prophet*

When we combine our life purpose with our gifts and passion, the outlet for it is work done as loving service. For many, that outlet is community service work. Through such efforts we not only help sustain our communities but we also grow in rich and unexpected ways. While it is important to be engaged in our communities through volunteer efforts, I want to focus this book on the work we do as our vocation. However, the ideas here can be applied to volunteer work as well. As mentioned in a previous chapter, those who find their calling and act on it bring their purpose into alignment with their daily activities, regardless of the area in which those activities take place.

Even if your vocation currently is not your calling, your work can be a spiritual endeavor. Spiritual work is work that draws energy and direction from a deeper source. When we call forth a power beyond ourselves to make our work flow smoothly, we tap into the Spirit of Life to sustain our work and guide our way.

Work can be a co-creative process with that deeper source within each of us. When we tap into this deeper source we achieve tremendous heights. But it is also true that when we tap into this deeper source we see the beauty and relevance of the tiniest and most mundane work. The following story shows how even simple work can be done in loving service to others and to God.

Hasidic Folktale

A bus driver sought the advice of the rabbi of Berditschev as to whether he should give up his occupation because it interfered with regular attendance at the synagogue.

"Do you carry poor travelers free of charge?" asked the rabbi.

"Yes," answered the bus driver.

"Then you serve the Lord in your occupation just as faithfully as you would by frequenting the synagogue."[1]

If we are to work spiritually, we must carefully examine what work means to us and how we can work with others in our organizations.

SPIRITUAL MEANING OF WORK

In the Judeo-Christian tradition, work has been described as either toil or fulfillment. We read in the Book of Genesis that Adam and Eve were cast from the Garden to toil and sweat like the beasts. Elsewhere in the Bible work is more positively described. In the book of Matthew, we are told to "let your light shine before men in such a way that they may see your good works."

I call that work "spiritual" when it speaks to a deeper sense of who we are and what we are here to do in the world.

From the sacred Hindu text, the Bhagavad Gita, we are told that "work done in the spirit of selfless service becomes worship." In Taoism work is no different than other aspects of our life; it should flow harmoniously from our center. The practice of Karma Yoga is based on the belief that work is an integral part of spiritual development. Through practicing Karma Yoga one comes closer to God through living life as an act of devoted service, even in the most mundane tasks.

Throughout the ages various writers have provided ideas on what it means to work spiritually. The quotes below are just a sample of these ideas.

From the Christian theologian Thomas Aquinas:

"It is natural for people to love their own work, because we love to be and to live, and these are made manifest in our actions, and because when we work we see our own goodness."

From the Sufi mystic Rumi:

➤"Let the beauty of what you love be what you do."

From the Universalist minister Olympia Brown:

"Divine Love is expressed through our human work."

From the Hindu text, the Bhagavad Gita:

"Don't ask if you like the work, if it is creative, if it always offers something new. Ask if you are part of work that benefits people. If you are, give it your best. In that spirit every beneficial job can be a spiritual offering."

From Mother Theresa:

"Love has to be put into action and that action is service. Whatever form we are, able or disabled, rich or poor, it is not how much we do, but how much love we put in the doing."

From these various perspectives, it is clear that it doesn't matter whether our work is to create great structures or to keep the hallway floors shiny. Our work is done to glorify God in our unique ways. We do this by offering our work as loving service.

Work done as loving service also provides us the experiences to grow into whole people. Influential writers in this century have described the importance of work to living fully.

From Rudolf Dreikurs:

"The three life tasks, Work, Love, Friendships, may be regarded as representing all the claims of the human community. Ultimately, right fulfillment depends on the development of social interest and readiness to cooperate. Consequently if one of the tasks is evaded difficulties will sooner or later be experienced in fulfilling the others also."

From Joseph Campbell:

> "Where do we get our bliss, where does joy come from for us? Then go out and seek that kind of work or make it happen; create it."

From Marge Piercy:

> "The pitcher cries for water to carry and a person for work that is real."

What matters is that we see the contribution of our work to a greater spirit. It is important to find ways to use our gifts and share our passion to serve others. This must be done in alignment with our purpose and our spiritual principles and values so that we have a strong foundation for our work.

SPIRITUALITY VS. RELIGION

I call that work "spiritual" that speaks to a deeper sense of who we are and what we are here to do in the world. This book takes as a fundamental premise that we have a higher purpose for our lives. Not only is it important to find meaning for what we do, but to find work that serves a larger purpose than materially feeding ourselves. Our life quest is to discover who we are and to offer our spiritual greatness to others.

Working spiritually is not about proselytizing a particular religious belief or doctrine. There are many gates to the garden. Working spiritually is also not about imposing beliefs on others or reciting scripture for others to adopt. It is about allowing ourselves to grow to new levels of understanding and moving in the world in the best way that we know how. I do not advocate that people enforce specific religious beliefs in the workplace. People need to access their spiritual values in whatever manner works for them and allow others to work from their own place of spiritual guidance.

Spirituality involves seeing the sacredness of everyday life. Religion involves practicing a set of prescribed sacraments. Religion is belief in a set of creeds, spirituality is a way of being, acting, or relating to another in a sacred manner.

Many people are leery of taking spirituality to work because they fear others will try to impose their religious beliefs on them, or try to convince them their beliefs are wrong. For these reasons, businesses (and government) want to be devoid of anything related to religion. This fear comes from confusing *spirituality*, finding a way to live and work in a sacred manner, with *religion*, adhering to a specific set of beliefs or doctrines.

Some people feel uncomfortable mixing their spiritual lives with their work lives because they fear their spirituality will be somehow tainted by being involved with their work. Yet this is a grave mistake, for it cuts people off from those sources of greatest inspiration and insights. Our best insights and creativity happen when we are most fully whole and aware.

When we work spiritually, it is like adding turbo charge to our work. We bring more energy, insights and care for our work. When we focus on those aspects of our life that lift us up to higher levels of being, we move further along our path for greatness.

Working Spiritually

The three words that I like to use to describe working spiritually are: wholeness, meaning, and connection. Many people work precisely to find wholeness, meaning, and connection in their lives. The artist or artisan who finds wholeness through creative expression is practicing spirituality at work. The engineer or scientist who tries to solve problems at work finds a sense of meaning when the heretofore incomplete pieces fit together and the problem is solved. The teacher who finds joy in nurturing the learning and growing process is practicing spirituality at work. The supportive co-worker who provides a kind word or gentle smile brings spirituality to the workplace.

The notion of "living your bliss" is a good description of what it feels like to find meaning and purpose in your work. The story of the three Masons illustrates this.

The Brick Masons

> When the first man was asked what he was building, he answered gruffly, without even raising his eyes from his work, "I'm laying bricks." The second man replied, "I'm building a wall." But the third man said enthusiastically and with obvious pride, "I'm building a cathedral."[2]

A hot business topic in the 1990s was to see other members of your organization as your "internal customers." This is a good first step in recognizing that how we treat our co-workers is important. But working with others spiritually goes much deeper than providing good customer service. It means recognizing and honoring co-workers as spiritual beings. For some of you, that may mean seeing the divinity in others, finding the light of God within them. For other readers that may mean recognizing the inherent dignity and worth of those with whom you work. Whatever perspective you take, when we see ourselves and others as spiritual beings our work takes on a different level of meaning. Every work encounter can be done to further our collective spiritual growth. We serve as ministers to one another.

In my work as facilitator for team building and planning retreats, I've used the spiritual concepts described in this book to great success. I've found that when people think, talk, and act in spiritual ways, they open up to tremendous levels of awareness, growth, and energy. I've also shared these ideas in presentations to civic and professional groups. Inevitably people thank me afterwards for bringing spirituality to the forefront.

What is important is that you see opportunities in your work to offer loving service to others. In so doing, you further your spiritual growth and support the growth of those around you. We must be aware and mindful of those opportunities to act in spiritually supportive ways when we might normally react harshly or judgmentally.

Some of our greatest insights happen through the most difficult times, but we must remain open to seeing our actions and the events in our lives from a spiritual perspective. Often the most difficult situations provide insight to our most important spiritual gifts or teach us new ways of being spiritual. Likewise, the most obnoxious co-worker can be our best spiritual teachers because they require us to go deep within ourselves for strength and understanding. As Jesus taught, it is easy to be kind to your friends, even tax collectors do that. To offer compassion to your enemy requires true forgiveness and strength.

Our spiritual foundation will strengthen as we recognize opportunities at work and in group settings to live out our spiritual principles. You don't need to remain in quiet blissful meditation or sit in silent prayer to grow spiritually. You can practice your spirituality at any time. Recognize that your spiritual journey continues at *all* times.

WORK SPIRITUALLY OR WITHER ON THE VINE

To think that spirituality does not play a role in our lives today and somehow is not impacting our work and organizational life is to deny the power of our spiritual yearnings. It is precisely in the busy domains of our lives that spirituality can emerge. Indeed spirituality *must* emerge in these areas or we will feel emptiness, senselessness, and despair that can lead to countless physical and social ills. Even those business leaders who accept that employee development is important to their company generally emphasize technical skills more than interpersonal skills. Rarely have managers seen spiritual growth as important to job performance.

There is a growing number of people who are searching for ways to integrate their spiritual life with their work life. People are fleeing the large corporate work environments because they want to establish work that is more fulfilling, or at least more flexible to meet their needs. Due to new telecommunication technology, many workers are no longer bound to sitting in a cubicle at work. But simply moving *where* we work will not result in integrating ourselves spiritually. We must find ways to have our work support our spiritual development and to see our work as integral to our spiritual journey.

In our modern era of instantaneous global communication, multinational corporations, and dwindling earth resources, we are challenged to find new ways of working and to create organizations that sustain our planet and support our personal and collective growth. Far too many people have become disillusioned and discouraged from working in today's corporations. Cutbacks and cost containment can lead to greater creativity and opportunities for growth when handled effectively, but more often the result of such events is greater anxiety and frustration.

Downsizing and off-shore labor result in many people looking for new jobs or making career changes. Job hunting can be viewed as a time for self-reflection and expansive thinking, but too often people feel dread and anguish instead. Those people who remain in downsized organizations often feel overworked and under-resourced. The efforts to squeeze every possible dollar value out of workers have left many people feeling exhausted and angry rather than enriched and fulfilled.

Yet work doesn't have to be a struggle, it can be an offering done in loving service to others. We must move from our fears and discouragement to find joy and purpose in our work. This shift from slow death to passion and joy will happen when we make the commitment to work spiritually.

It is essential for people to be intentional about working spiritually and to learn how to do so even when they are most stressed or distracted. When we find joyful expression of who we are through our jobs and in our organizations, we share our gifts and passion. When we see our work as a gift offered in service to the community and to serve deeper truths, we find a greater purpose for our work.

Working spiritually involves seeing our tasks and daily interactions as an opportunity to proclaim the divine, within us all and beyond us. It is in the fulfillment of ourselves in our work that we find and serve God.

EXERCISES

1. Write down as many words as you can think of that represent what spirituality means to you. Now write down as many words as you can think of that represent religion for you or that you consider to be "religious" words. How does religion and spirituality differ for you?

    Review your spirituality list and circle the words that you want to cultivate in your life. Now underline those circled words that you feel you can bring to your work or apply at work. Go back to this list periodically and see if you choose different words at another time.

2. Ask yourself: "How do I want to grow spiritually?" Write or draw your answer to this question in whatever shape or form your answer comes forth.

    a. Now think of ways that your workplace can support your spiritual growth.

    b. Are there people at your workplace who can be teachers for you? Who can support you in your journey?

Several recent books have been written about spirituality at work. Ones that have been useful to me are:

The Reinvention of Work by Matthew Fox, *Take Your Soul to Work* by Tanis Helliwell, *Wisdom at Work* by Let Davidson, and *True Work* by Justine and Michael Toms. See also the reference list at the end of this book for further reading in this area.

PART II

BRINGING SPIRITUALITY TO YOUR WORK

5

CREATING NEW METAPHORS

*As we let go of the machine models of work, we begin to step
back and see ourselves in new ways, to appreciate our wholeness,
and to design organizations that honor and make use of the
totality of who we are.*

—Margaret Wheatley, *Leadership and the New Science*

METAPHORS AS MENTAL MODELS

Most people are familiar with the classic Charlie Chaplin
movie "Modern Times." This movie depicted the
changes in work and society brought forth by the industrial
era. Too many people today feel they are merely a cog in a
wheel. The "cogs in a wheel" metaphor depicts people's
feelings of alienation and disempowerment in organizations.

This metaphor influences the way many managers and employees view work. They see their work as a cog in a larger wheel in which they have no influence. Similarly, many people don't they feel they can impact the wheel (their organization), and/or they feel that they are running ever faster to keep the cog moving.

Organizations are indeed interwoven systems with people performing different tasks that make up the whole. Organizational consultants increasingly have emphasized teamwork to create greater productivity. However, many people still have an individualistic view of work, and many reward systems in organizations are structured for individual rather than group accomplishments. Developing good teamwork skills takes a lot of training because most people haven't developed a team mindset, don't have sufficient interpersonal and communication skills, or don't understand group dynamics. I will expand on the topic of teamwork later, however it is important to recognize the view we have of work and to understand that what gets rewarded influences our productivity.

Metaphors are useful because they help us understand complex operations in simpler, everyday examples. Thus, metaphors can influence in a powerful way how we view aspects of our world. The "cog and wheel" metaphor has shaped people's view of work since the beginning of the Industrial Era. However, this is an incomplete and now outdated view.

"Man as machine" is a metaphor that has been part of our collective consciousness for several centuries. This collective consciousness is much more difficult to change because it is deeply embedded in the norms and beliefs instilled in our society and in many organizations. The norms and beliefs that are accepted as part of an organization's culture can be changed only with significant collective and sustained effort. Most research shows that making lasting changes in an organization's culture requires changing beliefs and norms at all levels of the organization. This includes beliefs held at a deeper personal level rather than simple compliance to new executive decrees.

Luckily, this metaphor is being replaced by visionary leaders who dare to create another picture. These top executives know that as the world changes, so too must our view of businesses. These visionary leaders understand that to be successful they must inspire personal excellence in their employees. In order to inspire such excellence, even if to do a simple but important task of cleaning an office, management must look at their employees as people with gifts to offer and creative minds to bring forth new ideas. Inspiring personal excellence requires another metaphor besides being merely a "cog in a wheel."

Top executives who know the value of creating a vision for their organizations are starting to help create new metaphors for work. Since organizational stories exemplify corporate vision, these stories are incorporated into the organizational culture. One good example of how the vision is embodied in the corporate culture is Southwest Airlines. The vision was simple, drawn on a cocktail napkin. The vision was to start an airline that would take Texas business travelers between Dallas, San Antonio and Houston, quickly and cheaply.

The story of how Rollin King drew a simple triangle on a cocktail napkin as he explained his idea to Herb Kelleher is told repeatedly throughout the company today. The cocktail napkin represents the company vision that has since lead to the company's expansion into 55 airports in 28 states by the end of 1999. The vision laid the groundwork. Their fight to fly within Texas, which ultimately was decided by the U.S. Supreme Court, resulted in the company metaphor of "warrior spirit." Today you will see pictures on the walls at Southwest headquarters in Dallas depicting the cocktail napkin and posters describing their warrior spirit. These are simple yet powerful images that inspire their staff to push the envelope and try new things.

Metaphors and stories provide us with mental images that help us understand our world. By adopting *new* metaphors, the beliefs and values of an organization are changed, thus affecting the organizational culture. New metaphors that help people feel empowered and view work as meaningful and purposeful go a long way in making organizational life more fulfilling and helping people on their path for greatness.

If we are engaged in our work at a deep heart level, then our work is truly sacrament; it accomplished what it signifies. Workers are grace givers, grace elicitors, grace granters in the community. The community is graced by our work.

— Matthew Fox

SPIRITUAL METAPHORS

Rather than accept separateness and alienation in the workplace, a new picture of wholeness and unity must be envisioned. The key is to create and promote new metaphors that will serve to empower people as well as to connect people to their work and each other. Positive metaphors for work can shift our perceptions from alienation and meaninglessness to seeing work and organizations as wholeness, meaning, and connection.

New metaphors for spiritual wholeness describe work environments in which integrity, authenticity, and compassion are present. In his book, *The Different Drum*, M. Scott Peck argues for bringing civility into organizations and uses the metaphor of organizations as community to bring about trusting and open workplaces that build more effective work relationships. Echoing similar views, Matthew Fox writes, "If we are engaged in our work at a deep heart level, then our work is truly sacrament; it accomplished what it signifies. Workers are grace givers, grace elicitors, grace granters in the community. The community is graced by our work."[1]

What would work and organizations look like if people acted with civility? Peck defines civility as involving a connection to a Higher Power. Various spiritual traditions have described this Higher Power using metaphors, since metaphors help give an image of the indescribable. In both Taoist and Buddhist traditions there is a belief that one must move with the flow of life, "letting go" of ego and desires, to achieve a higher state. There is a famous Buddhist expression, "Don't push the river, it flows by itself," which shows the metaphor of a Higher Power as the River of Life.

I am no more Messiah than you. The river delights to lift us free, if only we dare let go.

– Richard Bach, *Illusions*

In Richard Bach's book *Illusions*, he presents a wonderful parable using the metaphor of the River of Life. There is a river creature who tires of clinging to the rocks and stones and desires to let go and be set free. The other river creatures tell him he is a fool to let go, for the river will surely smash him against the rocks and crush him. The river creature decides to let go, for by clinging he feels he will surely die. At first he is smashed about by the current but eventually floats to the surface and learns to flow with the current rather than struggle against it. Further down the river he passes by other river creatures who see him floating, while they are clinging. Since he is a river creature like them yet he appears to be flying, they call after him "Messiah!" The river creature floats by saying, "I am no more Messiah than you. The river delights to lift us free, if only we dare let go."

Several Taoist texts describe leadership and peak performance using the "Way" as the flow of life. Jerry Lynch uses ideas from the Tao Te Ching in his book *Thinking Body Dancing Mind* to train peak performers to visualize what they want to achieve and open themselves up to the energy that flows within them to reach their vision. According to Lynch, the Tao Te Ching "teaches that each of us possesses a limitless power and potential that we can use and realize when we act in accordance with the forces of nature, when we align ourselves with the natural flow of energy or events. The Tao teaches us to react to life's circumstances by yielding, by not forcing issues or energies unnaturally, and by following the natural path of least resistance."[2]

The Art of War, written by Sun Tzu over two thousand years ago, is considered to be the most studied book on strategy the world over. The Japanese postwar business success is believed to be due in part to the wisdom taught by Tzu, that "to win without fighting is best." Sun Tzu's philosophy was that the ultimate use of knowledge and strategy is to make conflict unnecessary. *The Art of War* expresses the classic theme of Taoism – the less needed the better. The aim of generals is to have victory without battle.

The Tao of Leadership author John Heider suggests leaders move away from the traditional Western approach of controlling and manipulating followers. In the Taoist's paradoxical way, a leader must be selfless – there only to serve the group, and in this way serves herself. The leader teaches more through *being* than through *doing*, so must always remain focused on her inner truth in order to lead. A Tao leader knows that she must let go of control and allow the group to find its own way, comparing a leader to a midwife, there to help the process but never to force or intrude.

From the Tao Te Ching (no. 17)

The highest type of ruler is one of whose existence the people are barely aware....

The sage is self effacing and scanty of words

When his task is accomplished and things have been complete

All the people will say, "We ourselves have achieved it."

METAPHORS IN STORIES

The mythic journey is often used as a metaphor for facing challenges and overcoming struggles in our life. Perhaps the best known mythic journey is the search for the Holy Grail. In this story the hero, Perceval, finds the Holy Grail at the castle of the wounded Fisher King. He fails to ask the right question to heal the king and the castle disappears. The hero finds himself in the Wasteland to continue his journey. The wasteland represents the trials and tribulations of life. The hero must give up all he has achieved to find the Holy Grail again. Perceval is unable to find the Grail until he discovers his soul and transforms himself. Tanis Helliwell offers this interpretation of the Holy Grail story for corporate life today:

> We are both Perceval and the Fisher King – hero *and* victim. In our modern world, the Fisher Kings are the psychically and spiritually wounded individuals who run many corporations and governments, and who are creating a Wasteland of the Earth. None of us is innocent. If we are sacrificing both our body and soul to the desires of our personality, we wound ourselves. When what we do is not in accordance with the greatest good, we create a physical and spiritual Wasteland.

> To heal ourselves and our world we must ask difficult questions. However, like Perceval, we might neglect to do this. In learning to fit into the laws of society, we sometimes lose the power to see or speak the unadulterated truth. Only by

speaking the truth can we restore ourselves and our world to health. "Whom does the Grail serve?" (Does the personality serve itself and the material world or the soul and the higher good of all?) This is the question we must seek to ask *and* answer.[3]

A well known Native American story, Jumping Mouse, found in the book *Seven Arrows*, tells of a mouse who is willing to let go all that is known to find greater fulfillment. The character of Jumping Mouse is a metaphor for the journey and transformation that is possible for all of us.

In this story, a field mouse hears the roar of the river and seeks to find out what produces such a powerful sound. He goes to the river and is urged by a frog to jump to see the Sacred Mountain. When he jumps he sees the mountain in the distance. Even though the mouse lands in the water after his jump, he is elated by the vision of Sacred Mountain. Jumping Mouse returns to his family to tell them of his discoveries. Because he is wet and matted from being in the river they think he has been eaten and spit out by an animal. They see this as a bad omen. Jumping Mouse decides to leave them in search of Sacred Mountain.

Along the journey, Jumping Mouse receives the assistance of two animals that are sick and can be healed by receiving one of Jumping Mouse's eyes. In the end the blind mouse reaches the top of Sacred Mountain and must make one last jump to be transformed into Eagle. This story tells a classic mythic tale of a wanderer who faces hardships to find a greater glory, but along the way must give up those things that are most precious to him. Jumping Mouse is a story of how we find the power within us to conquer our obstacles to reach our visions.

From these various parables and metaphors we understand our life journey better. In order to correctly see the challenges and find resolutions we must be willing to look deeply at those things we cling to that prevent us from moving forward. Likewise, in work, we must carefully examine our behaviors and beliefs that hold us back from experiencing our greatness. We must stretch for solutions and ways of being that require us to transform ourselves. New metaphors for work will help us see work in a different light and help us see how we can work differently.

CHILDHOOD METAPHORS

Whether we are aware of it or not, we all have metaphors and mental models about work and life. Many of these metaphors come from early experiences and influential people. My grandmother was a great storyteller. One of her favorite stories was *The Little Engine that Could*. I can still hear her describe the little engine saying, "I think I can, I think I can" as it struggled to make it over the hill with all the toys for the children below. That story was her way of telling us not to give up if we found a task that seemed too great.

A close friend struggled to get through medical school because she was at the same time working through many painful early childhood experiences. Here is an example of a metaphor she used to help her finish medical school. Lyn decided to spend a week hiking the Appalachian Trail in North Carolina. On the hike she had an epiphany. Lyn realized that she needed to get to the next shelter hut on the trail or else she would end up sleeping in the woods unprotected.

Most of her life to that point had been movement to one of her "psychic" shelters, either staying at one shelter or venturing out and turning back because the way seemed too tough. She learned that she would be all right if she got caught "out in the woods at night" between the shelters. Lyn faced her fears and learned that she didn't need the "shelters" she had constructed that kept her from moving on. As a result, she went back to school and finished with more confidence and energy than she ever thought possible.

Sometimes our mental tapes or metaphors no longer serve us, are ineffective, or are outright unhealthy. Peter Alsop, a children's songwriter and prevention advocate, has a metaphor for many people raised in dysfunctional families. He says people develop armor to protect themselves from the emotional or physical abuse they receive. With each new attack and pain another layer of the armor is added, but the memories of the painful events and emotional wounds remain as swords deeply embedded in the armor.

Thus people learn to move in the world wearing many layers of armor covering the pain and preventing the hurt from coming forward into awareness. These people expend enormous amounts of energy just to get through the day wearing the heavy coat of armor and take very contorted postures as they move in order to avoid the swords still sticking in them. Unfortunately too many people won't take the time or expend the emotional energy to take the swords out. It is too painful to confront the experiences from which those swords left their mark. Some people prefer to walk through life contorted and weighed down, swords still deeply embedded. What a powerful metaphor that is for so many people's lives.[4]

Many companies don't foster supportive environments in which people can be trusting, open, and honest with each other. In too many companies people wear their armor and masks tightly. To become whole and connected, people must shed their armor and masks. What would it take to remove the swords and shed the armor? It takes courage, determination, and guidance. It also takes a lot of support from others who know there can be a healthier way to live. By seeing the armor metaphor and deciding to replace it with another more positive one, people can choose to move and work in the world differently. Many people's work would flow smoother and they would get along better with co-workers if they didn't have to carry their armor or avoid their deeper swords. How many people do you work with or know in organizations who wear such armor?

The stories above show various metaphors and provide descriptions for spiritual growth that allow us to face our fears and find our wholeness. Through our work, such wholeness can take form. In Chinese, the word for business (shen yi) can also refer to "meaning of life/living." It is through our business or work that our lives have meaning. However, our work is not just determined by our own efforts, rather it is influenced by the organization as well. Some people find they can not stay in organizations that don't allow them to live fully who they are. Unfortunately, too many people stay and die a slow death, too discouraged to see opportunities to be co-creative. Others feel they are in a position to transform their organizations so that people can find meaning in their work. New metaphors are needed, both personally and organizationally, that support our co-creative process. Several exercises are included at the end of this chapter to help you create personal and organizational metaphors that will serve you.

> *Sacramental work serves the cause of the Great Work of the universe, a work of interdependence and compassion.*
>
> — Matthew Fox

ALTERNATIVE METAPHORS FOR WORK
AND ORGANIZATIONS

Luckily, some new metaphors for work and organizations have been proposed that let us view work in other ways than the machine metaphor. These metaphors suggest ways to live fully through our work and be co-creative with the Divine.

73

Matthew Fox suggests a metaphor for work – that of a Sacred Sacrament. A sacrament as Fox defines it is "a holy revelation of the hidden mysteries of the Divine – mysteries so sacred they require metaphor and symbol if we are to talk about them." [5]

Fox suggests work can be seen as a sacrament and that we can move between different sacraments. For instance, leadership can be seen as an ordination. We confer upon leaders certain powers and privileges, but with that comes responsibility for taking care of the group and bringing the group to a higher level of existence. Likewise, teamwork can be seen as a marriage. Each member comes with her own individuality and offers it to the team. Yet as with a marriage, the team will take on a life of its own that needs to be nurtured and maintained. Fox writes, "Sacramental work serves the cause of the Great Work of the universe, a work of interdependence and compassion."

One activity for beginning to see your work differently through metaphor is to envision an activity that you enjoy doing. It may be a hobby or interest that you pursue, (e.g., hiking, weaving, quilting, cooking, rock climbing, dancing, scuba diving, etc.). What you want to do is to create a spiritual metaphor for your work that reflects your work in a creative, passionate, meaningful way. How can your work or activities be viewed in ways that are uplifting and life-renewing? What other images do you have that are inspiring and energy-sustaining? Use these images to help structure your work or symbolize your work environment.

One metaphor for work is that of being in a play. Our work is the plot that we must follow, with various other actors and props used to make the drama believable. Our workplace is the stage on which we move and carry out the play. We co-create the scene with those people who are on the stage with us. When we see our work as a play to be acted out, we can choose to make the play a drama, a comedy, or a tragedy. It is up to us as actors, individually and collectively, to act out the play so that the ending isn't a tragedy, but that it serves our highest good. We choose whether or not to act in the play in ways that support our own and others growth. When we see our work and organizations as arenas or stages in which our personal growth takes place, we see more clearly our role in choosing whether we work as in a tragedy or for greater understanding and personal growth.

Some of the props and actors may change, and we may have little to do with those changes. At times, a director or stagehand makes changes in the scene for us. But the Producer is always there, ready to offer loving support and guidance if we are ready to receive it.

Another metaphor for work and organizations is one of a symphony or dance. The organization works effectively to the extent that each of the parts is orchestrated or choreographed to fit into a smooth flowing whole. Work is a creative process, with the music or steps flowing together to speak to something meaningful inside those who participate as well as observe. The dancers or musicians are trained in their own work but must coordinate their part with that of the whole. Executives need to understand the deeper calling that is being brought forth from the staff and move them together in harmony. Anyone who has worked in a group where the energy and ideas flow easily knows exactly what jazz musicians feel when they are "in the groove."

Get a clear picture in your mind of doing an activity you really enjoy doing, one that gives you renewed energy, fills you with passion. Now imagine your work as if it were that activity or in the setting of the activity. Imagine who would be there assisting you, who else needs to be involved? What type of equipment or materials do you need? How can these materials or people be represented in your work? What feelings do you have as your work takes on the flow of this favored activity?

METAPHORS FOR ORGANIZATIONS

In his book, *The Different Drum*, M. Scott Peck describes his work in building community in organizations. "Organizations as community" is a useful metaphor to see our work environments in a more dynamic way. According to Peck, there are four phases involved in creating community. Moving through the stages of Pseudo Community, Chaos, and Void into True Community, work groups and executive teams come to a new understanding of themselves and their co-workers. This helps them to openly address problems, communicate honestly, and work through conflicts as they arise.

Tom and Kate Chappell also use the idea of community with their company, Tom's of Maine, Inc. According to Tom, an organization is analytical and hierarchical, whereas a community implies connectivity. Employees want to feel part of a community, not an organization.

"Organization as community" is an effective metaphor that leads to a particular way of seeing relationships in the workplace. The emphasis is more on personal connections. It must be supported by *real* practice and not just by having corporate slogans of "we're a family, we're a community" that are empty words. Treating an organization as a community takes dedication and energy.

New metaphors for work must include a long-term view of desired outcomes such as personal and professional growth rather than nanosecond results and quarterly gains. This long-term growth involves learning new ways of relating to one another in the workplace. It involves seeing each other as creative, dynamic people capable of growth and service.

In a recent study by the American Society of Training and Development (ASTD), they found that those organizations that grew significantly in both size and profitability were also those that invested more in training and development of their staff. The average training and development expenditure across industries was 2 to 3% of their budget (with some businesses investing almost nothing). The high-growth companies invested approximately 5% of their budget on training and development. These organizations knew that investing time and money into building their staff professionally would be a key to their growth and success.

My organizational consulting business includes teaching the "hard skills" required in today's workplace. Rather than referring to developing interpersonal skills as "training the soft skills" they really are "hard skills" to master, yet are vital to everyday workplace decisions and activities. How easy was it for you the last time you had to forgive someone for doing something that made you angry or let others down? Forgiveness and compassionate understanding involve very hard work. They don't come easily for most of us.

Organizations can be places in which deeper personal learning takes place. In fact, when people have gone through deeper learning and personal development, work is done much more smoothly and easily. Organizations are not just learning organizations for the sake of the company's bottom line. They can be learning organizations for the positive development of the individuals involved as well. But to do this, organizational members must be intentional about being open to learning from their mistakes and one another.

Another metaphor to use is the "organization as garden" metaphor. We see our work as gardeners tilling the soil and tending to the plants that will later bear fruit. Along with our co-workers, we use a number of tools to work the soil, each in our own way. Different departments grow numerous crops, and multiple gardens are tended simultaneously. In seeing each other as gardeners who bring different tools to the garden and who produce various crops, we think of and respond to the workplace differently. With the garden metaphor, people can experiment with the best ways to bring their crops to fruition.

For I know the plans I have for you, says the Lord. They are plans for good and not for evil, to give you a future and a hope. In those days when you pray, I will listen. You will find me when you seek me with all your heart.

— Jeremiah 29:11-13

All employees, not just managers, must tend to the collective garden of "healthy work relationships." By tending to this garden, better work environments are produced. Another benefit of being a gardener of healthy work relationships is that we develop and expand our interpersonal tools.

Any one who has gardened knows that timing is critical. Planting the seeds too soon or too late results in the plants never taking root. Likewise, projects must be timed right so as not to be harvested too soon or too late. Tending to a garden takes continuous care. Whether tending a garden or tending to community, the fruits are borne only if people are willing to invest time and emotional energy in the effort.

Peter Senge and other management consultants propose that organizations become "Learning Organizations." In this way, a metaphor for the organization could be a university. In Senge's book, *The Fifth Discipline*, he describes the process and benefits of organizations becoming learning environments. With the ever-changing demands of the marketplace and competition, organizations that can't adapt will wither and die. The adaptation process is one of ultimate flexibility and learning. When organizations see themselves as learning arenas, they create structures, policies, and processes to support learning. Organizations that build reward systems for learning see failures as part of that learning process. Rather than punishing failures, learning organizations promote experimentation and risk-taking. In this way, organizations will be most adaptable to change as the conditions of the industry demand. Learning organizations take to heart the adage "If at first you don't succeed, try, try again." They not only encourage risk-taking but also know the importance of discovering what is learned from failures.

These new metaphors must fit the needs of our time and promote our growth to wholeness. New metaphors provide us with images to understand the role that work plays in our life and what role you play in the life of your organization. What types of metaphors you use for work are limited only by your imagination. The key is to develop metaphors for work that inspire you to use your gifts and passion and that help you see the inter-relatedness of your work with others.

EXERCISES

1. The Seven Dwarfs "whistled while they worked." What stories or songs do you know about work being joyful? What messages were you given about work when you grew up?

2. Interview people you admire for balancing work with other aspects of their lives. How do they view work? What metaphors do they have for work?

3. Visualize your ideal work environment – what smells, sounds, sights, feelings, etc. come to mind. Hold this thought until you get a clear image of what this workplace would be like. Use this image and think of an object or scene or character that you can use as a metaphor for your ideal workplace.

   a. How would work be structured?

   b. Bring to mind your current workplace. How can you move it to your visualized ideal workplace?

6

AFFECTING CHANGE:
"LIVING AS IF"

*The language of this age must be concerned with the awakening
of vast multitudes to the possibilities rather than the limitations
of life.*

— Norman Cousins, *Human Options*

From the time of Enlightenment starting with Descarte and Newton, scientists were trained to believe there was an external world apart from humans that could be empirically measured and tested. This objective reality existed independently of the observer. However, current lessons from physics and psychology are challenging the traditionally accepted view of objective reality. Science and mystical traditions are converging in the belief that "the world is what we think it is," in other words, there is no objective reality apart from our subjective interpretation of our world.

Even memory and recall are shaped not only by the way the information was initially stored, but by what cues trigger the memories. Cognitive social psychologists examine mental schemas and personal experience that filter and bias the way all new information is processed. This field of research examines people's social construction of reality. Numerous studies on eyewitness testimony have found that when people must recall events they give different descriptions and judgments based on the words used in the lawyers' questions.[1] For example, when asked how fast a car was moving when it "crashed" vs. "bumped" into the other car, people give different assessments. A group of people may witness the exact same event yet give very different descriptions based on their physical and mental point of view.

There is a phenomenon well known to educators and psychologists called the "Self Fulfilling Prophesy" or "Pygmalion Effect." Various studies in classrooms have shown that when a teacher believes students will succeed or fail, they teach according to that belief. This in turn influences how the students view themselves, thus fulfilling the prophecy that they are dumb or gifted. It is because of this phenomena that some educational leaders disapprove of labeling students for special instruction. The "self fulfilling prophesy" works in all group settings, and thus business leaders and managers must be aware of how they project their beliefs about others' abilities.

Linguists have debated whether there is a concept separate from language, or whether a concept exists only after there is language to describe it. The typical example is from cultures that live primarily in snow. An observer not familiar with snow may only describe 3 or 4 types of snow yet to the native culture there may be a dozen types of snow. How many types of snow are there? It depends on who is describing it. Our mental schemas that sort information are influenced by our past experiences.

Well known in psychology is the concept of learned helplessness. This phenomena was first studied in animals that were placed in environments where they couldn't escape an electric jolt or other noxious stimulus. After being continually trapped in such an environment, the animal learned to give up and not try to escape. When placed then into a new environment where they could get away from the shock, the animal didn't search for a way out, it simply sat passively taking the pain. Their mental schemas and experience tell them they have no way out. People may live for years believing in the barriers that hold them where they are. The barriers become self-imposed.

Mystical and Shamanic traditions long have understood the power of the mind to create new realities. In many cultures, a Shaman is a healer who uses specially trained powers to see "the future healed Higher Self" of the ailing individual and bring that vision into reality. In the Hawaiian Huna tradition, the first principle is that of "Ike," meaning "The world is what you think it is." The remaining six principles expand on this concept. In the Huna tradition, all life is energy, and energy flows where our attention goes. Therefore, to create the world we want, we must be aware of our beliefs and our intentions to channel our thoughts and energy accordingly. All power comes from within and needs to be focused in the present moment.

Various metaphysical and mystical traditions teach that there are multiple dimensions of reality beyond the physical three dimensions. In shamanic traditions, the Dreamtime is an important dimension of reality. By traveling to the Dreamtime dimension one can experience other realities that are useful for the physical "waking" reality. The Dreamtime offers a place and time to learn from elders or interact with others so that greater knowledge and wisdom is shared and brought back to the "wakened" 3-D reality. The Dreamtime is not considered "unreal" simply because it is experienced in a non-waking state. It is just as real as our waking state, and the experiences one has in the Dreamtime affect our "conscious" reality. New insights and healing come from recognizing and appreciating the power of the Dreamtime as another form of reality.

An individual can take initiatives without anyone's permission.

– Buckminster Fuller

Great social and technical advances throughout history arose out of people's ability to see what is not present but what is possible. John F. Kennedy challenged the world with his proclamation that the U.S. would use its brainpower and channel its resources to do what had never been done before, put a man on the moon. It happened because enough people believed that it could be done. Similarly, Churchill envisioned a harbor at the beach in Normandy on which to put 100,000 troops. This harbor was critical for the invasion of Normandy. Since Churchill could see clearly a completed harbor at the site, despite those who questioned the project, after two years it became a reality. Who would have believed in the mid-1980s, during unprecedented nuclear missile buildup in Europe, that only a few short years later people would walk freely from East to West Berlin and the Soviet Union would no longer exist. Holding a vision of "what can be" is also important in less dramatic situations than these examples. Margaret Mead is often quoted in this regard: "Never doubt a handful of individuals can make a difference. Indeed, it is the only thing that ever has."

When the collective consciousness of a society focuses on a single idea, it can become a reality. The "hundredth monkey" phenomenon, as described in Ken Keyes' book of the same name, occurs when enough people have a shared vision or idea that it becomes a reality. The reality is created not just because people make it so but because it becomes part of their collective consciousness and world view. Many deeply engrained institutions we don't question today result from changes in our collective consciousness. Slavery is one such example. Though slavery was a common aspect of many human societies for thousands of years, few societies today tolerate slavery. Our consciousness has shifted such that our societies no longer see other humans as slaves but as inherently free people. Luckily, we have evolved to a higher level of being. At the same time, we have more evolving to do before we reach our greatest potential as spiritual beings.

"Living as if" involves having a clear vision of the reality you want to create and keeping focused on that reality enough to make it happen. It goes beyond the technique of "fake it 'til you make it." "Living as if" means truly believing that the end product or new idea can be made a reality. The course of action you take depends on you believing that what you want to create is *already* available. You need to live as if it were evident in the present. As one minister friend pointed out, the present is "pre-sent." With each step of "living as if" you bring that future reality closer to being manifested. When you act as if there is abundance, you start to notice abundance and see it in your life. When you live as if you are compassionate, you offer compassion whenever you get a chance.

Business leaders know the importance of believing in what can be done, even if it doesn't exist as part of present day reality. Many an opportunity has been passed by because people didn't believe in the visionaries' ideas. Stories of people who succeeded in the face of naysayers teach us to believe in our dreams to make them a reality. Lee Iaccoca held tightly to his belief that Chrysler could be turned around. He did this in the face of many skeptics who thought it couldn't be done. The "Wet Blankets" below seem almost ridiculous today since we take these "new" ideas for granted.

Wet Blankets Through History

· "This 'telephone' has too many shortcomings to be seriously considered as a means of communication. The device is inherently of no value to us." Western Union internal memo, 1876

· "The wireless music box has no imaginable commercial value. Who would pay for a message sent to nobody in particular?" David Sarnoff's associates in response to his urgings for investment in the radio in the 1920s

· "Who the hell wants to hear actors talk?" H.M. Warner, Warner Brothers, 1927

THE POWER OF VISION

Numerous books have been written extolling the virtues of visualization as a technique to develop greater creativity and enhance performance. Many of today's great athletes have trained themselves not only physically but mentally. They know how to visualize the success they want to bring about. In the winter Olympics it is common to see bobsledders visualizing making every turn successfully, ice skaters reviewing their jumps in their minds, skiers mentally preparing every turn in the snow. By visualizing the turns, jumps, and moves, the image of the correct motion is practiced in the body as well as the mind, so that mind and body act in unison.

Similarly, visualizations are powerful tools in expanding thinking and building creativity. Many management training sessions are done with executives and business leaders to teach them how to visualize what they want to accomplish. The biggest challenge to corporate leaders is to make that vision so clear to others that the path to the final reality is known and accepted by all. In this way, the collective consciousness of the organization moves the process along.

Stephen Covey prescribes the habit of "Begin with the End in Mind." This approach, like that of the shaman who sees the future Healed Higher Self, is useful in clearly visualizing what you are trying to accomplish and setting out the steps to get you there. Do not fall prey to the Alice in Wonderland approach – "If you don't know where you are going, any road will take you there."

As described in the last chapter, the metaphors used in work and organizations shape not only what type of work gets done but also how it is done. The mental images brought forth from the metaphors serve as templates for organizing tasks and building relationships. The next step after choosing the metaphor is to "live as if" the metaphor were true. If you see work as a dance, you will be more fluid and look for the pattern of the movements of others. If you see work as a sacrament, then the tasks take on new meaning for a larger purpose.

One young entrepreneur started her career working in the mail room of a publishing company. She had a vision of what she wanted to do in five years and systematically built upon that vision. She intentionally "lived as if" she were in the position one step higher than where she was (in how she dressed, acted, spoke). Within four years she had achieved the position she wanted and shortly thereafter left the company to start her own business and is now a successful magazine publisher.

By following what you love, you can "live as if" that way of life is true for you right now while you are taking steps to bring forth that future reality. In the best seller *Do What You Love, the Money Will Follow*, Marsha Sinetar describes a process similar to this entrepreneur's experience. Sinetar cautions that the money may not follow right away, and so people need to be realistic before they jump into a new venture. Most people have a hard time clearly visualizing what they want to do and an even harder time doing the mental work to move past the self doubts and mental blocks. As the wet blankets above demonstrate, there are enough naysayers in the world to hold people back from ever following their dreams.

Inventions and new ideas are created in the mind's eye first. Often it comes as a flash of insight, sometimes it comes more subtlety as in a dull sensation or nagging feeling. Developing intuition involves paying attention to those nagging feelings and brief insights enough to hear or see other clues through the daily mental chatter and rush of activity. Remember that you are co-creators of your experiences with Spirit. When working in conjunction with Divine Spirit, you sharpen your skills of intuition and increase the frequency of deeper insights.

Through activities such as prayer, journaling, and progressive visualizations, our visions and insights take form more clearly. You bring forth that which serves your highest good when you remain open to your inner wisdom. Similarly, if you continually visualize what you want to create, you will be surprised what kinds of information, people, or events you draw to you, bringing you closer to what you desire. Remain open to chance occurrences for they may bring you exactly what you need.

Through discernment, determination, and patience, what brings you passion can be your way of life. However, there will inevitably be sacrifices along the way as the story of Jumping Mouse illustrated. The sacrifices may be physical ones, such as trying to live with less for a while. More than likely there will be emotional or mental sacrifices that involve giving up comfortable or deeply held ways of thinking about yourself or the world.

"Living as if" is a process of being clear on what it is you want to create and thoroughly examining the potential consequences of such a new reality. Many people say they want to lose weight, but when they examine their motives they see that losing weight may mean spending more time exercising or giving up comfortable patterns of behavior. It is common in Weight Watchers meetings for dieters to express confusion or concern over relationships that change because the dieter literally has taken a new form.

BEING PRESENT TO THE NEGATIVES

By "living as if," you visualize what it is you want to create and live as if that state of being exists in the present moment. The focus of your energy, thoughts, and beliefs are on what you want to create in the present moment. Not long ago, I lost my wallet on a Friday afternoon. I knew if I didn't find it within a few hours, I would not be able to replace my drivers license or get any more money until Monday. When my wallet didn't turn up by the end of the day, I decided to enter gracefully into the zone of unknown – who had found it, what would they do with my credit cards, how hard was it going to be to manage without any identification or money for the weekend? I literally didn't have 20 cents on me.

This was a real challenge for me, and I knew very quickly that this missing wallet was a test from Spirit placed in my life at a meaningful time. Could I accept that I had done such a stupid thing? Could I surrender my fate to Spirit? Could I totally trust Spirit to provide for me until I put the symbolic, yet tangible pieces of my life back together? I had to release attachments. I prayed.

Luckily, a friend came to visit me that weekend who is a deeply spiritual person. She also could see this episode for the test that it was. We did a manifestation visualization for my wallet returning. I envisioned it glowing with such love and energy that if it was left on the side of the road someone would notice it and pick it up. I envisioned it being so filled with love that if someone had it and wanted to take the money or use the credit card they would think twice about doing so.

By Monday morning there was still no wallet, so I took the morning to call the various financial institutions to take care of things, went to the Department of Motor Vehicles to get a new license, bought a new wallet and went to my bank for cash. Though the morning was thrown off by having to run around dealing with this, I accepted the situation and didn't get mad or fume about the hassle and wasted time.

When I got to my office later in the day there was a message on my machine from someone who had found my wallet on the side of the road over the weekend. She said she would hold on to it until I could pick it up. The money and credit cards were all there, nothing had been taken.

I don't know what the lesson was for the person or persons who had my wallet over the weekend, but the lessons for me were clear. I had to enter into the situation with grace and surrender. This may seem like a small episode and may not trigger too many fears or concerns for some people. I know for me, even a few years ago, I would have lost sleep and stomped around mad for most of the weekend. Luckily, I had learned to accept the experience as an opportunity to trust Spirit and to release attachments.

Some people fear living in the present because they can't see past a present life that is too scary or too difficult. Living in the present moment may bring up past traumatic experiences or confront a present reality that is too threatening. Too many people seek refuge from a past or present life situation that is painful by escaping into excessive drinking, eating, sex, or work. Even if we want to avoid our "shadow side," we have to exert an enormous amount of energy to escape it. The old expression "you can run but you cannot hide" is true of the inner and outer dragons we must confront.

People develop defense mechanisms purely to avoid the harsh realities of life. At times these defense mechanisms (e.g., denial) can be very useful. But more often than not, the mechanisms are used long past the time when they are needed. Unfortunately, most people have practiced these defense mechanisms so well that to give them up would feel like losing a major part of who they are. Without discovering new ways of being to replace the outdated or unhealthy patterns of behavior, people will feel stuck. Unfortunately, resistance causes persistence. Or to put it another way, people would rather "deal with the devil they know than the devil they don't know."

More often than not, one's defense mechanisms are used long past the time when they are needed.

Rather than avoiding the unpleasant realities of our daily lives, we need to bring them to our awareness and accept them. Before we can slay our dragons we must be aware of the power they have over us. Too many times people do not want to accept their dark side. It is important to learn to release the self-judgments, usually in the form of self-criticism, or worse as self-defeating thoughts, as much as they need to confront the dragons that evoke them. Through time and practice it is possible to enter the darkness within and release the heaviness we carry.

Many people believe they are unworthy beings, having learned these lessons early in life. Too often people self-sabotage all their efforts or set out to prove how unworthy they are. In order to live as if you are healthy or prosperous or worthy, you first need to let go of the mental tapes that block you from believing it is possible. Sometimes these tapes are so deeply entrenched that professional help is necessary for us to recognize them.

Some people adopt a "Balance Sheet" approach to life. They believe that they get the good with the bad, and so they avoid good things because they live in fear or worry while they wait for the bad events that are just around the corner. We must learn to take life as it comes and not worry what else may happen, for we never know if it will be for good or not. As the heroic journeys of Perceval and Jumping Mouse teach us, we must go through struggle and lose what we hold dear so that we may be transformed.

In Susan Jeffers' book *Feel the Fear and Do it Anyway*, she provides examples and exercises for people to examine the fears that block their creativity and abundance. Unless we are willing to face our fears, we will never be able to "live as if." There is always risk involved. Many people find that the payoff of living in a spiritually whole and meaningful way is worth it. In order to bring forth the life that we want, we must be willing to live as if it were possible.

"Living as if" to affect change means setting your intentions to what you want to create. Learning to be co-creative with God, to ask that the greater good be done, allows us to see our power to create our world. However, we may not always get what we want in the form we ask. We have to remember that we sometimes can't see the bigger picture at the time. We need to be clear of what we want and then stay open for the grace of God to enter our lives. In this way we stay open to the life lessons that come our way.

In order to affect change, you must face the uncertainty and inherent dangers involved in the new way of doing or being. Letting go of the fear of the unknown and making yourself vulnerable to new possibilities is a critical element for any new growth to happen. "Living as if" is a powerful technique to gain confidence and courage to go through the unknown and vulnerable time. To "live as if" we must have a clear vision of what we want to bring forth and ask that our journey forward be done for our greatest spiritual growth.

EXERCISES

1. If you "lived as if" you had a certain job or had the kind of relationship you want or other dreams for your life, what would you gain and what would you potentially lose? Are you willing to accept what you gain and give up what you may lose?

2. Here are some spiritual "living as if" questions to ask in any situation, particularly when you need greater guidance:

    · Am I "living as if" the choices I make or the actions I take create a more compassionate world?

    · Am I "living as if" what I did mattered?

    · How can I "live as if" I am growing towards wholeness?

    · How can I "live as if" there is social equality?

    · Am I "living as if" there is abundance (of love and other resources I need)?

    · How can I "live as if" I honor myself and others with true acceptance and understanding?

3. Find a metaphor in this chapter for work or your workplace that you would like to bring to the present. Imagine what it would be like to go into work next week if the metaphor were true. Make two columns on a piece of paper with headings for each column "Positive Consequences" and "Negative Consequences." First list out all the negative consequences of "living as if" your metaphor were true. Then list out all the positive consequences

of "living as if" your metaphor were true. Do you see ways that you can overcome the negative consequences? How do the positive consequences help you "live as if" it was true?

Other resources for ideas provided here:

Gawain, Shakti *Creative Visualizations: Use The Power of Your Imagination to Create What You Want in Your Life*, New World Library, Novato, CA, 1995.

Chungliang, Al Huang, and Lynch, Jerry *Thinking Body, Dancing Mind: Tao Sports for Extraordinary Performance in Athletics, Business and Life*, Bantam Books, NY, 1994.

7

LIVING INTENTIONALLY

Life is a song – sing it
Life is a game – play it
Life is a challenge – meet it
Life is a dream – realize it
Life is a sacrifice – offer it
Life is love – enjoy it

– Sathya Sai Baba

Intentions are the basis for action. What we intend to do is a powerful indicator of what we actually do. In fact, research of the relationship between attitudes and behavior show that behavioral intention is the best predictor of actual behavior. Intentions are the broom that sweeps the way for the actions to follow. Intentions put us in the right frame of mind and get us focused on what we are actually going to do.

Our intentions help us obtain our goals. According to Adlerian psychology, all behavior is purposive and goal-directed. Our early life goals shape how we view ourselves in the world (e.g., as competent, powerful, fearful, or powerless). Some goals may have been appropriate in earlier stages of life but are not healthy now. Many people have developed goals to succeed at any cost, to hurt others who hurt them, to protect themselves from being hurt, or to show others how powerful they are. These goals must be brought to light and re-examined to determine if they are ones worth keeping. You must be intentional about your goals.

It is easy to see how goals operate at work because most of us spend time every year, if not every week or month, developing goals. We then set out to structure our time and resources to meet those goals. Yet it is often difficult to see our goals in interpersonal relationships, and rarely are we aware of them as we interact with others. Living intentionally involves seeing clearly our goals in work and relationships, indeed at all times.

Living intentionally is the antithesis of our contemporary escapist culture. Rather than avoiding unpleasantness in our lives we must enter into our confusion or hardships. Only then can we make choices about how to deal with them. When people in your workplace annoy you, a natural reaction is to hide from them or wish they would go away. Be aware of what *you* do when you interact with them and how you contribute to the conflict. You can choose whether to support or change your patterns of behavior that contribute to the dynamics. Though you can't change someone else, you can choose how you will relate to her. And by changing your behavior you will affect your relationship with her.

You must be intentional in order to live freely rather than be enslaved by your past experiences or habits. We can not have free choice to determine who we are and how we want to live if we are not intentional. Once we "live as if" something were present in our lives, then living intentionally is the next step to bringing it into reality. Living intentionally means being aware of the goals we have and determining whether these goals are in line with living a spiritually-centered life. Living intentionally means taking responsibility for our lives and seeing our roles as co-creators in it.

LIVING INTENTIONALLY AS CO-CREATORS

In various mystical traditions, the intention carries with it the energy that creates reality. If we put forth an intention of doing harm, even if we don't physically do harm, we have done harm at an emotional, spiritual, psychological level. One needs only walk into a room where a fight is about to break out to feel the energy there. Even if no physical actions are taken, the energy creates damage to the relationship.

Similarly, we know that in sexual encounters even if no action is taken the intention creates an energy between two people that is easily sensed. Thus, any intention put forth by the thought of acting in a certain way sends out specific energy.

Some traditional and most alternative medical professionals understand the mind-body connection in this way. We must set the intention to heal and focus on healing rather than be subsumed in our illness. Constant worry about our illness only puts more thought and energy into the illness. Continual attention and focus on healing and being stronger provides our body with energy to bring about greater health. Fighting an illness is not the same thing energetically as creating healing.

Shamans and mystics through the ages have used intentions and directed energy to heal and transform reality. In the book *Urban Shaman*, Serge Kahili King explains the use of creative intuition. By tuning into intuition (in some traditions called divination) and making it available to the conscious mind, reality can be transformed. The third principle of "Makia" in the Hawaiian Huna tradition (energy flows where attention goes) teaches that it is important to focus on what you want and be present in the moment to draw forth the desired object, thought, or feeling. In other shamanic traditions, intentions help bring forth what is desired by making it manifest from another reality.

Visualize a recent encounter with a co-worker that was difficult. Now think of your intention as you began the encounter. Were you angry and did you want to get even with someone, were you frustrated and wanted action, were you hurt and wanted some support, were you taken off guard and wanted clarification or protection?

Get a clear picture in your mind of what you wanted before, during, and after this encounter. Hold those intentions clearly in your mind and determine if they are intentions you want to keep or change.

If you want to change the intentions from hurtful to helpful intentions, visualize yourself as a loving spiritual being, capable of forgiveness, understanding, and compassion. Reflect on how you feel as a forgiving, compassionate person. Feel the warmth of Love come over your body and through your mind. Release judgments of being right or wrong. Hold the image of you as a caring, compassionate, understanding person.

Visualize the other person as a loving spiritual being. See her inner divine light and watch it expand and grow brighter. Imagine she is growing and developing into her more Loving and understanding self. Visualize her as whole, helpful, and supportive. Hold your awareness of the other person as a spiritual being just as yourself.

Create an intention about how you will act towards that other spiritual being next time you encounter her. Make the intention one that supports and affirms who she is (e.g., I see you as a caring person, I understand why you are acting that way, I accept you as a divine spiritual being). Write out ten positive intentions towards that person on separate index cards. Review and rehearse those intentions once a day for the next week. When you encounter that person during the next week, live out one or more of those intentions.

I have had so many experiences in the past 15 years as I've learned to be co-creative with God that I no longer see these events as "just coincidences." I know if I stay open to finding what I need and ask for support in creating it, I draw that experience to me. I must trust in the grace of God so that I can become an instrument of peace. I usually preface such intentions with the phrase, "May the Highest Good be done," knowing full well I can't always see in that moment what the greatest good is. In other words, we can create our reality through our intentions, though it might not come in the form we ask.

As mentioned earlier, my husband and I left our jobs to travel overseas for 6 months. That in and of itself was a leap of faith, yet we knew that our next phase of life would unfold for us as we needed if we stayed open to it. During our trip, on several occasions when I needed something, it manifested itself. As we were leaving Australia to go to China, moving from summer to winter, I realized I'd need a warmer jacket. Since we hadn't budgeted for buying a jacket, I set the intention to find something that would help me stay warm. On the last night in Sydney, I opened a drawer in our hotel room and found a thick sweater left by a previous traveler. I used that sweater for our time in China and then left it in Bangkok at another hotel for whomever might similarly need it. Later in Germany when I needed more warmth, I found a jacket in a hotel room, and again I used it for several weeks then left it for another traveler before we left for home. I set the intention of finding something to keep me warm and I was able to do so.

On the same overseas sojourn I visited a monastery in Thailand. While spending the next day in silence, I got the vision of having a bracelet or wristband that would represent my spiritual journey. I didn't get a specific representation other than a multi-colored woven bracelet. I thought it likely I would find such a bracelet in a street market somewhere.

The next night a Canadian woman we had befriended stopped at our bungalow to say goodbye since she was leaving early in the morning. We exchanged addresses and took photos. Then on her way out she said she had presents for us. She produced two beautiful brightly colored woven friendship bracelets she had made for us. I was stunned when I saw it because it was similar to what I had envisioned. I wore it for the remainder of my trip.

Another episode that demonstrates how our intentions support our ability to "live as if" was when I was in between jobs and feeling the pinch of money. I wanted to attend a workshop that cost $30 and I just didn't feel that I could afford to go. Since I felt the workshop would really help me during that time, I called the workshop leader to see if I could pay a smaller amount. He was generous enough to allow me to pay what I could afford. I attended the workshop and loved it. When I got home that evening, I checked my mail and found a birthday card from my grandmother. My birthday wasn't for another couple weeks but her check of $30 came at just the right time!

LIVING INTENTIONALLY AS MINDFULNESS

Living intentionally means being mindful of what you think, feel, and do at all times. It means being aware of the present moment and knowing that how you think, feel, and act in the present moment is all that there is. It means embracing all that comes to you in life and then *choosing* what aspects of your life you will give power to through your thoughts, feelings, or behaviors. Living intentionally means choosing how you will live and taking responsibility for your choices.

Probably the person most responsible for bringing the term "mindfulness" to our country is the Vietnamese Buddhist monk Thich Nhat Hanh. His books, such as *Miracle of Mindfulness* and *Being Peace*, help us gain more clarity and focus in our hurried lives. These books speak to a deeper yearning in our Western culture to release the stress and struggles of daily living. We are too often struggling to catch up with ourselves. Most people find there aren't enough hours in the day to get basic chores done, let alone think of spiritual growth. Yet Thich Nhat Hanh's books are so valuable because he shows us how to be mindful in our typical, hurried, stressful lives.

Mindfulness can be practiced at any moment, with various cues commonly found in our busy lives. When the phone rings at work, let it ring an extra time and bring your mind back into awareness of your surroundings and breathing. When you go to get a cup of coffee, think of where the coffee was made and be mindful of those people who were responsible for bringing that coffee to your cup. When you are at a stop light, instead of getting angry at being delayed, use the time to bring your awareness back to your body and notice how your body is reacting to your feelings.

Mindfulness can happen with every breath. Thich Nhat Hanh's books include wonderful short chants and poems for bringing your mind back to awareness of your surroundings with every in breath and out breath. These can be done in less than 30 seconds. My favorite one of his is, "Breathing in I calm my body, Breathing out I smile." The key is to be aware of your feelings, your body, your breathing, and to let go of the attachments that disturb your mind so you can think clearer and listen better.

For many people, their mind is usually five steps ahead of their body, and even further ahead of their inner feelings or spirit. Thus, the mind can get impatient with the body and spirit, resulting in disharmony, even dis-ease. Slowing down the mind and body allows time to be more focused on the present moment. *You can't live fully if you don't live in the present.* If the mind is always in another place and time, you are not living in the present.

Here are some other short phrases to help center you and keep you focused on the present moment.

I dwell in peace (in breath)
I offer peace (out breath)

At this moment (in breath)
I am strong (out breath)
With each breath (in breath)
I am whole (out breath)

Hundreds of people have found comfort and support from saying the Jesus Prayer – "Lord Jesus have mercy on me." People say it as a chant or recite it repeatedly. You can say this also in a short breathing meditation:

Lord (in breath)
Jesus (out breath)
Have mercy (in breath)
on me (out breath)

You can think of numerous simple breathing affirmations that help you set your intention when you are working or feeling stressed. They help calm you down and regain your focus.

I particularly like a breathing meditation from the Sikh tradition that translates as "Divine Teacher Within, I call upon Thee." The meditation is offered here as a yoga breathing meditation in the original language.

Ong   (breath in through the left nostril closing the right nostril)
Nämo   (breath out through the right nostril closing the left nostril)
Guru Dev   (breath in closing the right nostril)
Nämo   (breath out closing the left nostril)

I learned this breathing exercise from Gurujodha Singh Khalsa. He is the corporate counsel for the Khalsa International Industries and Trade. Gurujodha and other top executives of Khalsa International start each day with 30 minutes of yoga and breathing meditation. Their company offers time during the day for yoga and meditative practice for any employee who wishes to participate. The executives at this company believe such practice allows their staff to think more clearly and to be more open to one another throughout the day.

I learned another good yoga breathing exercise from an American Sikh businessman. This can be used as a focusing meditation. I've adapted it a bit here for your use.

> Let the seed in my heart – (in breath)
> Be planted out into the universe – (out breath)
> Let the manifestation of ecstasy – (in breath)
> Turn now into divine wisdom – (out breath)

Periods of quiet alone time (even 15 minutes a day) are important to slow down the mind and bring your body into harmony with your mind and spirit. Through prayer, meditation, journaling, or physical activities such as yoga, tai chi, jogging, swimming, or bike riding, people have found they can slow down their minds enough to be aware of their breathing and to take note of how their body is feeling. More importantly, this quiet reflective time allows you to open yourself to guidance or insight on problems you want to resolve. A spiritual teacher once said "If only I could pray for 8 hours a day, I would get so much more work done."

Visualize a situation recently where you were in a difficult or stressful situation. Take a moment to recall how you felt during this event (e.g., was your body tense, were you uncomfortable, was your body weak, or were you on edge). Let these same feelings come back to you as they occurred at the time.

Now breathe deeply into your body. Taking several deep breaths let your breath flow to all parts of your body – legs, feet, hands, head, stomach, shoulders. With each inhale, send new energy to that part of your body that is most uncomfortable. With each exhale, release the tension or stress from your body. Send it away with your breath, knowing that you no longer want it.

AND NOW A WORD ABOUT LOVE

Living Intentionally ultimately requires that we "live up to our divinity." This is no small task, in fact it *is* our life's quest. As the quote from the beginning of the chapter said, "Life is a sacrifice – offer it, Life is love – enjoy it." Living Intentionally means finding that place inside of you where your inner light is located. It may take years for some people to discover their inner light (some people have more layers of armor to dig through), or a much shorter time for others. Living up to our divinity requires that we discover that Light Within and then remain continually focused on it to guide our actions and words. This light is Divine Love.

But what exactly do we mean when we use the word Love? Love is often misunderstood. Love is used so frequently in terms of romantic love that it is difficult to reprogram our understanding and use it in any other context. And in fact, when in the presence of a spiritually loving person, it is easy to feel an attraction that too often is attributed to romantic or sexual attraction. Charismatic leaders have experienced this confusion amongst their followers. Likewise ministers have been trained to distinguish Higher Power Love from romantic or sexual attraction.

In English we don't have enough words to describe the various types of love. In Greek there are three distinct love words: "Eros" meaning erotic or romantic love, "Philia" meaning brotherly love, and "Agape" meaning compassionate love.

Agape love is what I am referring to here. Many religious traditions speak of God as Love. Following the path to greatness means discovering that Spirit of Love inside of us and offering that Spirit of Love in service to others.

Kurt Vonnegut gave a talk titled "Love is Too Strong a Word."[1] He told how he and his wife were painting a room in their house and were struggling with it. At one point his wife turned to him and said, "I don't love you anymore." Vonnegut replied "that's OK – you will again in a few weeks." From this story, he explained that if we must always feel love for another we will feel we constantly fall short. Of course, his meaning of the word love was more of a romantic notion. He preferred to use the term respect rather than love. Vonnegut said that if his wife had turned to him and said she didn't respect him anymore, he would have been concerned.

"Live as if" there is abundance and Love in your life, and you will bring it forth.

The other familiar concept of love is that of a parent for a child. But unfortunately, for too many people this type of love is distorted. Many people have been raised by parents who used love to manipulate or control their children into behaving as they wanted, accepting or rejecting their children as suited their desires or fulfilled their needs. This type of conditional love is not the type of Love I am talking about either. This type of conditional love should not be used at work or at home because it is another form of coercion.

When I talk about spirituality in the workplace, I am ultimately talking about Love. I can hear some objections now "Whoa – we can't have love at work. That would be distracting; we'll bring in all sorts of sexual harassment charges," or "The business world is all about competition and beating out the other guy. This love stuff isn't suited for business." But let's look deeper into what we mean when we talk about Love in a spiritual sense. We're *not* talking about romantic attraction, we're not talking about being gushy or soft. Sometimes the most loving thing you can do to someone is to tell them they need to find another job.

I am talking about Spiritual Love, which requires forgiveness, compassion, and strength. Spiritual Love as described in the New Testament and the teachings of Jesus is referred to as Unconditional Love, Pure Love, or Christ Consciousness. This type of Love in Buddhist traditions has been translated as Loving Kindness or Compassionate Understanding.

Martin Luther King Jr. used the Christian framework of Love to bring Gandhi's non-violence tradition to America. Through the belief that we are all God's Children and that "power over" is not the way to live, King showed us how strong Spiritual Love can be.

> When I speak of love I am not speaking of some senti-
> mental and weak response. I am speaking of that force which
> all of the great religions have seen as the supreme unifying
> principle of life. Love is somehow the key that unlocks the
> door which leads to ultimate reality.[2]

Offering compassionate understanding or loving kindness doesn't mean we must agree with what others are doing. Even when we firmly believe people are not acting in helpful or healthy ways, we can still offer them loving kindness. Through our actions, words, or intentions we can model compassionate understanding.

Spiritual Love requires us to accept our own and others' frailties and to know that we are all on a path towards wholeness. Unless we accept our own imperfections, we will never accept them in others. We can use the times of imperfections as "teachable moments" for ourselves or others involved.

The Dalai Lama's approach to oppressive regimes is to extend loving kindness in the face of hostility and thus, by example, he shows another way to resolve conflicts.

So, for example, even when thinking about those Communist Chinese who inflicted great harm on some of the Tibetan people — as a result of my Buddhist training I feel a certain compassion towards even the torturer, because I understand that the torturer was in fact compelled by other negative forces. Because of these things and my Bodhisattva vows and commitments, even if a person committed atrocities, I simply cannot feel or think that because of their atrocities they should experience negative things or not experience a moment of happiness.[3]

(A Bodhisattva is an "awakened warrior" who acts out of love and compassion to attain full Enlightenment for the benefit of all beings.)

Similarly, Martin Luther King Jr. writes:

The nonviolent approach does not immediately change the heart of the oppressor. It first does something to the hearts and souls of those committed to it. It gives them new self-respect; it calls up resources of strength and courage that they did not know they had.[4]

Everyone can offer compassionate understanding, even when they most strongly disagree with someone. Again, in the words of Martin Luther King Jr.:

Compassion and nonviolence help us to see the enemy's point of view, to hear his questions, to know his assessment of ourselves. For from his view we may indeed see the basic weaknesses of our own condition, and if we are mature, we may learn and grow and profit from the wisdom of the brothers who are called the opposition.[5]

Gandhi taught the concept of Ahimsa and Satyagraha. Ahimsa was the term given for his non-violence practice and is an essential part of Satyagraha (Sat = truth, Agraha = firmness). Ahimsa is "a firmness of truth that guides action." When one bases all action on the search for truth, there is strength and power involved rather than weakness and submissiveness.

The teachings of Gandhi, King, and the Dalai Lama have been instrumental for scores of people to learn how to be change agents through the principles of Spiritual Love. From their life examples, it is clear that Spiritual Love can move deeply entrenched systems and bureaucracies. Thus, Spiritual Love can be used effectively to create change in the work place (to create healthier or more productive work environments). Spiritual Love can be applied to the workplace when people are intentional about practicing and learning these basic principles.

When you need to make a decision, particularly if it will affect others directly, ask, "What would Love do now?" This is just as appropriate in the workplace as anywhere else. Business decisions and work activities are behaviors by humans that affect humans; therefore, the same principles hold. When asking what would be the Spiritually Loving thing to do, you need to reach deep into your inner wisdom for guidance.

There are powerful stories of entrepreneurs and CEOs who used the principle of love in order to grow their business. In his book, *Reawakening the Spirit in Work*, Jack Hawley tells the story of how Isaac Tigret, founder of the Hard Rock Cafe, built the chain to be the smashing success that it is by using a company motto "Love All, Serve All." He even decided to put short love aphorisms on the back of T-shirts they sold such as "Start the day with love," "Do good, be good, see good."

Tigret didn't start his restaurant in order to make millions of dollars, he started it to close the gap between social classes in England. He started his business to serve others, the profits came as a byproduct. The company motto didn't just apply to customers. Tigret ensured it applied to his staff as well. In fact, he broke strong traditions in England by paying women staff the same rate as men. He describes how the work environment felt when the company motto was applied.

"Everybody loved the place, everybody felt bigger working there. We were famous. Just walk into the place and this great energy hit you immediately. Employees were proud of the place, from the dishwasher on up."[6]

It should be clear that the everyday use of the term "love" will not suffice when speaking of working spiritually. Another form of love must prevail. This form is based on wholeness, compassion, truth, and forgiveness. It is important to adopt a meaning for Love that resonates with you in order to offer Love, whether at work, in meetings, with family, or towards yourself. You must recognize and honor the source of Spiritual Love within yourself. When you seek to nurture and support it in others, you will be well on your path for greatness.

EXERCISES

1. Think of a work relationship that could be improved.

    a. What intention do you have in that relationship? Is it based on fear, distrust, anger, discomfort, or is it one of helping, healing, compassion, caring? What loving intention can you create towards the other party?

    b. Visualize yourself in this relationship living intentionally in a way that supports and nurtures your own and the other's spiritual growth. Once you get that image clear in your mind, how do you feel in the relationship in this new way? What other intentions will you need to have to make the relationship grow into a Spiritually Loving one?

2. Write down in a journal, in as much detail as you can, your vision of how you could work in a comletely spiritual way. Now, instead of saying to yourself, "I want XYZ" to happen, every day for a month write down what you will say, be, or do to make that vision become reality. This will help you focus on living the future ideal state you wish to create.

8

SPIRITUAL GUIDANCE

Find the spirit deep inside
Find the spirit on a mountainside
Find the spirit in a rushing tide
Find the spirit in your heart.

— The Washington Sisters

I was fortunate enough to have a minister as a spiritual mentor during a stressful time in my life. At one point when I was dealing with a broken relationship and sitting in her office crying, trying to sort out how to get through the emptiness, she asked me a profound question, one I was not expecting and it stopped me suddenly. Her question was, "What does faith have to do with this?"

Since at that time in my life I was an avowed atheist, the question at first didn't make any sense to me. I think I just stared blankly at her while I tried to comprehend the question. The first thought that rushed through my brain was "I don't believe in a God, so how can I have faith?"

I knew she had a reason for asking the question and I trusted her judgment to guide me through this experience. I took the question seriously. I stammered out an answer, "I guess I have faith in myself, faith I'll get through this period." Just saying these words made me feel better. It helped me see that the darkness and sadness I was feeling wouldn't last forever.

Having faith in something is a huge first step in knowing there is a solution to the situation. Just knowing there is a solution is enough to give you hope. With hope, you can begin to see possibilities that you didn't know were there.

Often when we are depressed or confused, our whole outlook is so bleak and dense that just lifting the fog a little bit can give us the energy to move forward. Finding that opening in the darkness is what it takes to begin to steer ourselves out of the hole we find ourselves in. Grace is amazing. "I once was lost but now I'm found, 'twas blind but now I see" are powerful words. We've all been there before. Being open to faith and open to spiritual guidance is important for moving from confusion and uncertainty to hope. The hope we find when we see through our darkness is enormously freeing.

OPENING UP TO GUIDANCE

I was lucky to have a minister who could be my spiritual mentor during that time in my life when I was sorting out careers and relationships. It is greatly beneficial to have someone who can ask you the right questions and help you sort through your answers in a supportive and non-judgmental way. Find those people who can assist you in your journey. As the Buddhist saying goes, "when the student is ready the teacher will come." As you open yourself up to growing and learning more spiritual ways of being, you will recognize others who can provide insights and model a spiritual way of living.

Through my work with Rev. Laurel Hallman, and later with friends who were also growing along their spiritual path, I was able to learn how to get connected to my Source for greater guidance.

I still need instruction, ideas, and reminders of how to get back in touch with my Source, but it comes easier to me now. Practice is important. You must actively maintain your spiritual practice. Part of your spiritual practice is to be open to receive insights or affirmations in your journey. I have often found that songs help me open up to my Source. Hymns, chants, and various songs help me remember that Spirit is available if I can find a way through the darkness or confusion to be open and connect to it.

One of my favorite songs to cheer me up when I'm feeling blue is a song by the Washington Sisters called "Find the Spirit." The verse I particularly like is the following:

> Some people say that the spirit is under a roof and four walls
> Open the door on Sunday morning, close their door on
>   Sunday afternoon
> How would you feel closed up? We all need the sunshine
> Carry the spirit with you every day
> It'll teach you to fly.

Too frequently we are bombarded by chaos in our lives and feel burdened down rather than able to fly. During these times it is hard to hear answers to our queries and find the clarity we seek. In these times, it is important to find a calmness in the clatter.

Whether you do this by saying a short prayer or singing a short hymn, it is important to get to a place of focus and centeredness. From that center you come back into balance like the wobbly doll that, when knocked over, always rocks back to its upright position.

Develop a short affirmation or blessing to help you find your center. Repeat these words when you are feeling stressed or need guidance. The words provided earlier, "Divine Teacher Within, I call upon thee," the Jesus Prayer, or any words of inspiration will help you regain focus and remind you to be open to spiritual guidance.

Most importantly, listen to, watch for, or feel the response. In the reflective mind or in the responsive body, you can get the messages you need to discern your direction. If you get a feeling or inclination to pursue an idea or action, take the initial steps and see where they lead you. In big decisions, you will need time to discern what to do. Ask Spirit for clarity and wait to receive the guidance in whatever form it takes. This requires patience and openness.

When I am uncertain about what to do, or if there is a hunch that I'm not sure whether to follow, I ask for guidance or affirmations. The affirmations may come to me literally or symbolically. I can usually tell within a few hours or a few days whether I was right in my actions. Here is an example of how I was able to get guidance and clarity about a job decision.

After nearly a decade of sorting through my ideals and values, I thought the only way for me to do all that I wanted to do was to work for myself as an independent consultant. But going out on my own and not doing the traditional 8 to 5 job was pretty scary. Some family members questioned whether I could do it. I trusted my intuition and kept open for an answer. At two different times I turned down what appeared to be good jobs for me. I felt something deep within say "no, this isn't right for me." The last time it happened I was convinced I needed to go on my own.

I was in the process of being hired for a job that seemed in most ways perfect for me. It would allow me to use a variety of my skills and somewhat set my own schedule. I really liked the man who would be my boss and felt it would be a fairly fulfilling job. But I've learned to listen to my body to help me determine if I'm on target or not. When I got really sick for two days, I knew I needed to pay attention to it. I called a friend who was a massage therapist and made an appointment. Her session was helpful for me to open up to my inner knowing. After her massage, I told her very confidently and calmly, "I know what I need to do. I need to start my own consulting company."

After I got home and told my husband of my decision, I went to the answering machine to check for messages. One of the messages was from a woman in town who had seen my resume. She called to see if I was interested in doing some consulting work for her agency. I just smiled as I heard her message. That was the affirmation that my decision was on target. The next day I called the man with whom I had been interviewing and told him I was going to start my own business. He was disappointed but understood my decision. I worked with him as a consultant on several occasions after that.

This is but one story of many experiences I have had that illustrates what it is like to receive guidance and be open to an inner knowing. When we see ourselves as co-creators with the Divine and ask for assistance to see more clearly what we need to do, we get the direction and affirmations we need. This may involve asking that the answer be shown to us in a dream, meditation, or prayer, through journaling activities, or even trance-like states from extended exercise such as jogging or swimming laps. The key is to remain open to receiving the idea or lesson being offered.

BEING VULNERABLE

People who want complete control of their lives never open themselves up to serendipity or the mystery of life. It is hard for these people to have faith in anything beyond themselves or to ask for assistance from Spirit. Yet to live and work spiritually we must be open to seeing and learning new ways of connecting to the Source. Instead of blocking out the grace of God from entering your life, open yourself up to it. This requires giving up control and being vulnerable. Rather than leaving you weak, being vulnerable is an important step to learning how to be co-creative with the Divine. It is a powerful experience when you connect with those who are there to assist you.

A minister once spoke about needing to give up control to welcome God into our lives. She asked us to see our life with God as a dance, where we allow God to be the lead and we follow. Rev. Diane asked us to be open to that dance by saying, "God, You and I shall Dance." She then showed the following on a placard:

$$G + U + I = DANCE$$

When we open ourselves to the dance with God we receive the guidance we need.

While I was writing this book I experienced vulnerability on many occasions. One situation provided an overwhelmingly positive affirmation. A man who had been dean of two reputable business schools came to my university to talk to our department about changes we could make in our curriculum for business majors. He met with each the faculty member individually, and when it was my turn to meet with him, I prepared myself for a fairly routine academic conversation.

He introduced himself and shared where he had worked and what kind of research he had done. I felt uneasy telling him my areas of interest because I didn't think the academic institutions were quite ready for professors to do work on spirituality in business. But I felt it was my calling to do this work so I told him about my book. Instead of criticism or derision for injecting such nonsense into management practice, I got an overwhelmingly positive response. He said he had wanted to write an article on the spiritually-integrated manager some ten years earlier but had never gotten around to doing it. For the rest of our hour-long meeting, we spoke of the need for more of such work to be done and how it could be brought into mainstream management arenas. I was totally unprepared for having such an affirming conversation. Had I not made myself vulnerable, this conversation never would have happened. He bolstered my belief that the time had come to talk about this topic in the classroom and in preparing the business leaders of tomorrow.

The most difficult part in being vulnerable is accepting criticism and risking failure. It takes courage and conviction to believe in what is right for you to do. When you see the abundance of experiences and learning opportunities, you know you can never really fail from doing something. The key here is to know that your experience will lead to greater growth if you look for the lessons of the moment.

Many people won't find their greatness because they fear failure. They worry that they will look stupid if they try something and fail; they feel they will let others down if they fail; they fear they will be harmed in some way if they fail. However, the only failure is in failing to try. There are countless examples of people who "failed" in an earlier life endeavor but are seen today as heroes or success stories. Abraham Lincoln "failed" in three businesses and lost in five elections before he became president. Thomas Edison was kicked out of school because the school master thought he was too stupid to learn.

A manager of a hospital emergency services department took the risk and made herself vulnerable by asking her staff for suggestions to improve her skills as a manager. In order to get honest feedback, she asked her staff to elect one person who would collect the suggestions and transcribe the comments so she would only receive a typed composite of ideas. This process resulted not only in her department being run better, but it built trust in her department and respect for her as a manager because she acted on the ideas presented. She took a great risk in soliciting her staff's response since she didn't know what they would say or whether she could make the changes they suggested. In the end, the payoff was enormous for productivity and employee morale. It also resulted in the manager improving her skills for long-term effectiveness. This manager's story is but one example of being vulnerable so that we can be of greater service.

You won't fall short of becoming your Highest Self when you live in a co-creative way with the Divine Spirit. However, this doesn't necessarily mean you always get what you want. Even if the outcome doesn't turn out as planned or desired, it can be a necessary step in your spiritual journey. In fact, some of the hardest trials and perceived "failures" are exactly what we need most to open our eyes to a better way of being. As the saying goes, "when God closes the door, He opens a window." Look for the openings in your life where your deeper wisdom can come through.

INTUITION AND DISCERNMENT

Often we only get vague notions about what we should do. We can either pay attention to these notions and act on them, or we can ignore them and push them aside as distractions. We must be willing to take risks and extend our comfort zones, to explore vague notions and see where they lead us. We do this sometimes out of curiosity, but more times than not, we build our intuitive skills as an act of faith. We don't know where our intuition will lead us, but we have faith it will be worth pursuing.

Through quiet contemplation and reflective discernment the answers we seek will emerge. Don't look for a thunderbolt "A-ha!" phenomenon. Usually we only hear a faint whisper or have a vague sense that we are on the right track. We must continually ask that our path be made clear and that we can more easily do what we are supposed to do.

I've thought about Rev. Hallman's question on many occasions, particularly when I've felt confused, frustrated, or uncertain. "What does faith have to do with it" also can be turned into "What does faith lead me to do now?" Living faith-fully often requires us to follow our gut feelings even without knowing where they will lead us. Acting on our intuition may feel like taking a leap of faith.

Building intuition usually comes slowly. In our society where "the proof is in the pudding," we usually need hard evidence before we will take risks. This is especially true in the business world. Before we feel confident that an idea is worth pursuing, we often gather lots of information and supporting evidence. Our rational approach to decision-making often overshadows those hunches we get that we're on the right track. It takes a lot of convincing of yourself or others to trust intuition, especially when the evidence is to the contrary.

Always prepare yourself, you never know when you'll be called to do great things.

— Abraham Lincoln

I want to be clear that I don't think it is wise to base most actions purely on hunches and intuition. The best approach is to find a blend of rational, logical thinking with discernment and intuition. Because intuition can't be objectively assessed it has been dismissed from being a valid form of knowing. However, rather than feeling you must choose *between* reason and intuition, recognize that they are both valuable tools.

There are numerous stories of scientists who have made great breakthroughs from intuition, or business leaders who followed a hunch, resulting in the product being widely successful. There are also plenty of times our hunches lead us to dead ends. To start to build your intuition, pay attention to the hunches and see which times they lead to a dead end and which times they pay off. As you begin to act on your hunches, in small ways initially, you will begin to see a pattern develop of times when it leads you astray or not.

On several occasions when I either took on a new consulting job or turned one down, I would get a sign or have a conversation that confirmed my decision was right on target. I've since learned to trust my intuition and allow myself time and space to discern what I need to be open to learning or doing. Our intuition emerges from uncertainty, but settles into our deeper knowing when we practice discernment and reflective living.

In *The Corporate Mystic*, Gay Hendricks and Kate Ludeman outline some basic ideas to cultivate your intuition, particularly how to sort out fears from intuition. It is important to be willing to face your fears to know how they are affecting your judgments. To hone your intuitive skills, you will need to distill when your inner voice is calling out of fear or when it is guiding from clarity. Often times we let our fears dictate what we should do, thus we pay attention to those inner messages that say "do the safe thing, take the path that's known." By letting go of our fears and being willing to trust our inner knowing, we open ourselves to new possibilities.

Intuition, like faith, grows with each new time we trust it and it leads us where we need to go. There are various techniques to practice discernment, including meditations, visualizations, journaling, Dreamtime awareness, shamanic journeying, vision quests, hypnotherapy, and silent retreats. I have used all of these practices at one time or another to help me get the clarity I've needed at different points in my life. If you are just starting to be interested in building your intuition, practice this discernment process simply and allow time to see what comes clear for you. Be patient and stay open to seeing it working in your life. Spiritual guidance comes in many forms – remain open to receiving it.

EXERCISES

1. What feelings, emotions, or cues do you receive when you know you are on target with an idea? What conditions will help you receive these signals better?

2. Think of the last time you took a risk. What gave you the confidence or determination to take the risk? What did faith have to do with it?

3. Are there any situations or events that you find yourself repeatedly facing? What do these situations show you about an area where you need to grow or change?

4. What messages were you taught early in your life about being "perfect" and about failure?

9

CREATING SACRED SPACE, CREATING SACRED TIME

Disciplined reflection does not take time away from work; it sustains the spirit and increases the intensity and quality of work.

– Keshavan Nair

How many times have you tried to start a project and just couldn't find the energy to get going on it? How many times have you found yourself thinking of three things at once and forgot what you walked in a room to do? How many times have you had a conversation with someone that was important but forgot what was agreed upon a day after the conversation? These are all examples of not living intentionally, mindfully. Creating sacred space and sacred time allows you to be more present, more mindful of what you are doing so you don't have to repeat the same conversation or work again. In the end, you will *save* time by creating sacred time and sacred space because you will be more aware of what you are doing. With practice, you *will* be more effective because you will be co-creating your experiences with Divine Love.

There is a traditional Buddhist story of a student who asked his Master about the Buddha nature. The Master replied, "Before the Buddha reached enlightenment he chopped wood and carried water. Afterward enlightenment, he chopped wood and carried water, but he did so as an enlightened being." This story tells us that our life may look no different when we live it spiritually. We still will do the day-to-day tasks we always did, but by working spiritually we act from a different state of being. Ultimately, our entire day, week, and life can become Sacred Space and Sacred Time. We become enlightened beings who do all our work in a sacred way.

CREATING SACRED SPACE

Social commentators focus on the breakdown of community – in other words, not having a Sacred Time or Sacred Space to gather and reconnect with one another. A few years ago, I had the opportunity to visit a young man who grew up in the former East Germany. He described how he and his friends would sit around and tell stories and create games to entertain themselves. After the wall came down, they were only interested in the latest movies and electronic gadgets of the west. He lamented that in the years after their openness to the west, his friends no longer took the time to share their lives with each other or be creative as they once were.

In his book *The Great Good Place*, Ray Oldenberg describes the breakdown in community and how important it is to have a place where people can gather. Many retired people gather in malls in the morning to walk and visit friends as a way of breaking their sense of isolation. Community building is only one aspect of creating sacred space. Most towns no longer have the corner drugstore soda fountain, and few people use the park benches and the city center to sit and discuss their lives. In fact, most cities have vagrancy laws that discourage people (particularly teens or homeless people) from gathering outside in public places. Traditional community gathering places have been replaced by video arcades and fast food restaurants.

The renewal of interest in coffee shops and salons during the 1980s reflect a desire to reconnect with others in our hurried lives. Traveling in Europe in the mid-1990s, I read about an effort started in Italy called the "slow food movement." It began as a backlash against the American fast-food lifestyle that was invading Italy. The slow food movement wanted to preserve the culture of taking time to enjoy good food, good wine, and good conversation.

Community building is only one aspect of creating sacred space. Think of a time when you entered a sacred space, perhaps an old cathedral, a place of worship, a beautiful place in nature. How did it feel? Usually there is a sense of peacefulness, a stillness. You may feel a higher state of awareness, Love, or increased energy in this space. However it feels, it is certainly a different feeling than our daily work environments, which are usually hurried, stressful, even unnerving. Creating sacred space means choosing a particular place where you will bring that same degree of awareness, peacefulness, and Love.

I had the privilege to facilitate a planning session at a retreat center in Virginia that was built and decorated with Cherokee themes. It had a seven-sided meeting room, similar to those used by the Cherokee for their councils. The walls were covered with tapestries made by Cherokee people depicting various stories of their heritage, stories of struggle and triumph. The energy of that space was tremendous. It seemed fitting that I start our day-long retreat creating sacred space.

I focused our ingathering by honoring the sacred hoop of which we all are a part. I "called the directions" to honor the spirit energy represented by the four geographic directions – North, East, South, and West. The general manager of the company told me at the end of the day that he attributed much of the success of the retreat to my ingathering. He felt it gave us a clear focus and inspired energy.

Sacred space can occur anywhere; you don't need to be at a special retreat center to find it. A doctor in one of my workshops said that during work in the emergency room she used to go to the bathroom periodically just to slow down her mind and get herself more focused and centered. After attending my workshop a lawyer told me she put up a screen in her office to create sacred space. She used this space to sit quietly in meditation when she needed to regain focus or clear her mind.

Choose one place somewhere in your daily or weekly routine where you can feel more spiritually connected. You may have to do a personal ritual or guided imagery to create this place as Sacred Space. This place may be your car as you drive to work, the bathroom down the hall from your office or your break room. Think of this place as your sacred space such that whenever you enter it you will release your worries, doubts, and anger, and draw in Love. In this space you can renew yourself to go forward with greater loving kindness.

For various consulting projects or meetings, I have done a guided imagery of the room where we will work as a sacred space. Below are several visualizations you can use before important meetings or projects. Take just five minutes of quiet time before you go to the meeting or go to the room before others arrive and try these.

Visualize the meeting room or work environment to be filled with Divine Light and Love. See the chairs and tables as props for your spiritual drama to unfold, serving as tools for your work. Visualize the people in the room acting in their Highest Divine Love, working together cooperatively, serving a common goal and Higher Purpose. Imagine the door as a gateway to Spiritual Love, and all those who enter it will feel the presence of this Divine Love. Create this space as Sacred Space in your mind and fix your intention on this sacred space throughout the meeting.

Another possibility is to visualize sweeping the room of any distracting or negative energy, sweeping all thoughts or intentions that block growth or the Higher Purpose in to a large white sack. Then visualize the sack filled with the thoughts and intentions that don't serve a Higher good bundled up with a gold chord and taken to another place where it will be held until the meeting is over or transformed in to a sack of loving intention and good will. Ask that the thoughts, intentions, and actions of the others involved be used for the Higher Purpose of the group.

Meetings are a source of tremendous wasted energy and time when people are not focused enough to contribute to them or the group isn't focused enough on the task. Creating a simple ritual to get the group to focus on the present and let go of what they were doing before they arrived can be enormously effective. Rituals in the work place can be done individually or as a group to help create sacred space. Try a simple moment of silence or guided meditation at the beginning of a meeting to allow people a chance to clear their mind of distractions and invoke a feeling of harmony and peacefulness. This results in the next hour being so much more productive.

On several occasions I have worked with people who were about to go into a meeting or group situation where they knew there would be stress, discomfort, or hostility. Through visualization or guided meditation, they were able to gain emotional strength and become spiritually grounded. This allowed them to deal with the situation through loving intentions and compassionate understanding. This practice focuses on bringing forth only loving intentions and releasing any fears, doubts, or thoughts that could block the Higher Purpose of the event.

It is helpful to sit face to face, with either eyes closed or staring at each other for 5 to 10 minutes while we do a guided meditation to help get connected to our Higher Power. Various visualizations can be used for this. One I especially like is to have people imagine a bright light (some think of it as the Holy Spirit) coming through the top of their head and flowing through their body, bringing in warmth, love, and compassion. They visualize this light clearing their body of stress, fear, or doubt, at the same time filling their body with Pure Love (Loving Kindness or Holy Spirit). In this way, they are more focused and can tap into their inner Light for guidance and strength that then can be brought forth in the meeting. As a result of this visualization people frequently say they got through the meeting in a much better mental state and accomplished what they hoped for or more.

CREATING SACRED TIME

A common response in my workshops on working spiritually is, "I just don't have the time to do one more thing." And my usual reply is you need to *make* the time. Of course, making time, squeezing one more thing into an already packed schedule, is never easy. But if this practice becomes central to all other things you do, you will be amazed at how easy it is to "fit it in." Once you bring Sacred Time into your normal routine, you won't be able to imagine living without it, the same as you couldn't imagine not brushing your teeth or going without your sacred cup of coffee in the morning.

Creating Sacred Time goes one step further than the rule of scheduling your priorities. Creating Sacred Time means understanding that the time you take to bring spirituality into your life is sacred and essential. You need to honor it and ask others to honor it as well. Honor this time not because you feel you "have to do one more thing," but because you deeply want this sacred time and you will function more effectively by having it. It

Creating Sacred Time means understanding that the time you take to bring spirituality into your life is sacred and essential.

allows you to live a soul-replenishing life. It means you treat this time as sacred and it cannot be violated. With sustained practice you will see most of your daily activities done as sacred time.

Unfortunately, in our hurried lives we've forgotten what Sacred Space and Sacred Time means. In fact, very little of daily life is seen as sacred these days. Social scientists have found that simply having a family dinnertime can be a great asset to positive youth development. The traditional time for the family to gather and discuss what happened during the day, reconnecting in the process, is lost in our hurried lives. Dinner time can be an important Sacred Time, to rejoin the family and refocus on Spirit. Creating Sacred Time to say prayers of thanks before meals or at bedtime is another powerful way to connect with spirit and one another.

In the Judeo-Christian traditions, the sabbath is the Sacred Time and the church or temple is the Sacred Space. The sabbath is a time of reflection and prayer to reconnect with God. It is also a time to reflect on what the rest of the week brought and what may come ahead. The sabbath was developed as an important time to renew the spirit, to rest and not "work." Participating in a Friday evening Seder Supper brings a sense that this is a special time, it only happens once a week, and it is a big deal. It is a time of reflection and connection, a time of prayer and thanksgiving, a time to honor God and one another in the family.

The closest secular holiday we have for this is Thanksgiving dinner. It is meant as a Sacred Time to reflect on our abundance and give thanks. But so much emphasis is put on the preparation of food and timing the meal between football games that the importance and sacredness of this holiday is lost. When was the last time your family sat down for a meal where the focus was on each other and renewing your spirit?

Practicing Sacred Space and Sacred Time is very difficult in our fast paced lives. There will be many trade-offs and sacrifices made in doing this. Merely having anything sacred in our lives today may be a challenge. But think of what you will be giving your children by having some time to get together as a family to connect with and honor each other, to thank each other for their contributions, and to thank God for your blessings. This time may be during a meal, on the drive to your house of worship, during a weekly walk around the block, or before bedtime. It could be anytime. The important thing is that everyone must understand that this time will not be violated, it will be kept sacred and honored. For those people not in a family, set aside the time as sacred time for yourself doing whatever you feel will help you be spiritually renewed, perhaps finding a friend who can participate in this time as well.

In his book *The Search for God at Harvard*, Ari Goldman described his challenge as a journalist to celebrate the sabbath. He described his inner turmoil over meeting his own spiritual desires to practice the sabbath given his work demands. He was able to get assignments that allowed him to have Friday evenings off. When he had to travel on Fridays he created his own sabbath on the road. The lesson of this book is that he found God in his struggle to keep the sabbath and he understood how important it was for him. We must all face that challenge as we juggle busy schedules. But again, the point is to make it so central to who you are (or how you want your family to be) that it becomes Sacred Time and Space – that it cannot be violated. You will make the sacrifices necessary to live this way because it is sacred, holy, and spiritually renewing to you.

Companies can honor sacred time by allowing people time to celebrate a sabbath. In the Muslim tradition, the sabbath is Friday, in the Jewish tradition it is Saturday, and in the Christian tradition it is Sunday. Thus, scheduling around people's sabbaths can be tricky. Several companies such as Chik-Fil-A aren't open on Sundays because they feel people should have one day a week to be with their families. Tom's of Maine is one company that struggled with scheduling work as their company grew. They didn't want to require people to work on the sabbath. They wanted to be respectful of the various sabbath days but needed to run their shop seven days a week, so they had to be creative in finding various shifts that worked.

Helping people honor their holy days is also something companies can do. One example of a company that made the effort to help an employee honor sacred time is Timberland Co. Jeffrey Swartz, CEO of Timberland, described an encounter with a sales representative for Timberland who was having a hard time keeping his normal work pace because it was Ramadan and he was fasting during the day (Ramadan is a Muslim month-long holy period). The salesman assured Swartz he would do his job, but he declared his faith came first. Swartz knew that Timberland would have to figure out a way to support this person so he could do his job. Swartz (a Jew) told the salesman's supervisor (an Anglican) that something would need to be done to help the salesman (a Muslim) be successful. This is a good example of how working spiritually isn't a matter of a prescribing a particular religious practice at work, or forcing someone to believe something they don't want to believe. It involves recognizing that people are spiritual beings and need to be supported as such.

SACRIFICIAL COMMITMENTS

Often times we must give up activities or obligations to honor those aspects of our lives that are sacred. I call these sacrificial commitments. Everyone should take stock periodically to answer this question: What aspect(s) of your life is/ are so sacred that you will sacrifice other duties to fulfill them? Probably one of the hardest things we can do is to schedule those things that are sacred to us and not allow other things to break our commitment to them.

I once heard a great expression that explains sacrificial commitment. "How do you spell love to a child? The answer: T-I-M-E." How often have we put off doing something with those we love because we have some other obligation demanding our time? When we see that the time we offer for sacrificial commitments to ourselves or others is an act of love, it takes on a whole new meaning and level of importance. By honoring our commitments to create sacred space and time we are acting out of Love.

Don't think of creating Sacred Space and Time as a New Year's Resolution, to be broken when the situation demands. It must be seen as a covenant with yourself (or with God) to honor this time or place and use it for your Higher Good. Seek out those who also wish to create Sacred Space and Sacred

Time and develop a pact with them to help one another honor your spirituality. Have a buddy system to help keep your sacrificial commitments.

Ask any artists about Sacred Space and Sacred Time and they know what you are saying. It is a time or space that they relish having, look forward to their whole day to spend time doing what they most desire doing. Many people may feel self-conscious about creating Sacred Space and Sacred Time and may worry what others will think. It is important to know yourself first and be clear on what is sacred to you.

Therefore do not be anxious saying, what shall we eat? or what shall we drink? or what shall we wear?... but seek ye first His kingdom and His righteousness and all these things shall be yours as well.

– Matthew 6:31-33

After traveling to the Middle East, I was impressed at how much religious practice permeated the daily life of the people there. I wondered how differently our work life would be if we stopped periodically throughout the day to bow in humility to Divine Creator and pray for our work to be done to serve a higher good. After I returned from that trip I made a commitment to offer thanks throughout the day for the many blessings I've been given. Now I take time at meals and at the start and end of each day for prayer. Though I've had to stop a business conversation when my food arrives during lunch or dinner, most people don't mind my practice and often comment that they would like to give thanks as well. Rather than feeling an outcast for taking time for this prayerful way, I've generally been supported for doing it.

The expression "to do something religiously" means exactly that, to be committed to something that is a holy practice. When you do something with this level of commitment, you feel whole and fulfilled by doing it, and empty or restless not doing it. Creating Sacred Space and Sacred Time means you couldn't imagine living without this time and space in your life. When your spiritual yearning becomes central to who you are, you will do it regardless of what else is going on in your life.

EXERCISES

1. What in your life is sacred? Why are these things sacred to you? How do you preserve them as sacred?

2. Look at a typical week or month and make a list of all the activities you do during that time. Which of these activities are important enough for you to consider them sacred? Now think about what activities do not promote (or actually get in the way of) your spiritual growth. What activities can you discontinue so that you will have more time for your spiritual development?

3. Write down 5 things that you can do to renew your spiritual energy and focus. Think of where and when you could do those activities. Who can you solicit for help to ensure you will do them?

4. Remember a time when you were in a Sacred Place, perhaps a temple or church, a forest or magnificent natural place. Bring back to mind what you felt, heard, smelled, saw in this place. Recreate the feelings of connection, awe, wonder, or peace, and feel it in your body. Now think of a place or time in your workday where you can recreate those same feelings. What can you do to create Sacred Space in your home or work environment?

Further reading on creating sacred time:

Reilly, Patricia Lynn, *I Promise Myself: Making a Commitment to Yourself and Your Dreams*, Conari Press, 2000.

10

HEALING FROM ADDICTIONS

That which is most important, hold most lightly.

– Buddhist saying

This chapter on addictions is an important one because addictions often come to light when doing spiritual work. They become obvious when people are intentional about their spiritual growth. Addictions cause enormous pain and injury to others and wreak havoc in the workplace if not fully understood. Organizational members must be aware of the challenges involved in spiritual work because it is not all sunny and joyful. Spiritual work requires reaching deeper pain and addressing your weaknesses.

When we bring our spirituality to our work, we see the intentions and actions of ourselves and others more clearly. As a result of this greater clarity, many people who are unaware of addictions in their family, their workplace, or in themselves, often see it for the first time. Thus, what often goes unrecognized as an addiction (drug, alcohol, gambling, work, technology, etc.) comes into the light. Healing any addiction is necessary to moving towards greater personal and workplace health and spiritual growth. This work is necessary to get over the boulders along your spiritual path.

Everyone must see their woundedness and take responsibility for moving past it. This is especially true for addicts and people working with addicts. Though most recovering addicts recognize they are powerless over their addiction, it is important not to adopt a victim mentality. We are all co-creators of our lives. Therefore, we must see what decisions and steps we can take to improve our lives. We must claim our power, not give it away or deny we have any. Sometimes our decisions are between the lesser of two evils. It may not seem like we really have any good choices to make. However, slowly over time, with each healthy choice we make, we can dig ourselves out of the unhealthy patterns we've established. It may take a decade or more to fully work through all the ramifications of the addiction. With perseverance and support, we can follow a path to greater wholeness.

I've seen friends and colleagues work through tremendous obstacles to follow a path of healing and ultimately become stronger lights for others. Many people don't see their woundedness or scars and so carry on as if they weren't there. Eventually the wounds will impact how you relate to others. Take note of times when you've struggled and look deeply at what your motives or intentions were. You'll likely see your actions came from a past wound that needed attention. Perhaps if you are struggling now with difficult life circumstances you are being called to seek greater healing. Do the work you need to do for your healing so that you may serve as a light for others.

As described earlier in this book, people have all sorts of armor that they wear to cover old wounds. Over time the armor conforms to fit the body so well that people often aren't even aware they are wearing such armor. Workplace armor consists of dysfunctional behaviors learned to deal with repressive or addiction environments. Through spiritual practice, this armor becomes noticeable and you see how it blocks further growth. In order to go through the healing process, as with other areas of your life, you must recognize your armor and begin to step out of it. You must remember to be gentle with yourself and others as you or they go through the healing process.

As your spiritual practice develops, you will understand how important it is to have authentic relationships and to be honest with yourself. Such authenticity prevents the dishonesty and deceit required for addiction to continue. Whether the addiction is manifested at work or in your personal life, it is important to know that your relationships will change as you unveil the deceit and see yourself or others as they truly are.

CHARACTERISTICS OF ADDICTION

Unless you've dealt with someone suffering from an addiction, you are unlikely to know how devastating it is to human relationships. It is important to recognize the characteristics of addiction and know appropriate ways for relating to co-workers with an addiction. From a spiritual perspective, this will require a lot of patience, tolerance, and forgiveness as the addict tries to come to terms with her condition. It will take professional assistance and several attempts for the addict to learn healthy ways of functioning. Rather than judging and blaming, it is important that co-workers walk the balancing act of providing support for the addict's growth and healing without engaging in behaviors that support the addiction.

How many of these norms and messages are supported in your organization?

1. Don't talk about problems

2. Don't express your feelings openly

3. Communicate indirectly through a third party rather than directly to those with whom you have a problem or issue to address (triangulated communication)

4. Be good, strong, right, and *perfect*

5. Make us proud

6. Don't be selfish

7. Do as I say, not as I do

8. It is not OK to be playful or to play

9. Don't rock the boat

These nine rules of behavior, outlined by Robert Stubb[1], are rules found in addictive families. It is interesting to note how many of these are similar to the Protestant Work Ethic and Victorian culture as well. It is not surprising that these rules are deeply engrained in the dominant American culture. As described by Anne Wilson Schaef in *When Society Becomes the Addict*, addictive systems occur throughout our society. Most people have learned and adopted at least some of these dysfunctional behaviors as a response to the addictions around them. These dysfunctional behaviors are then viewed as "normal" acceptable behaviors to uphold. Without spiritual awareness these behaviors become quite damaging to our society.

Dysfunctional behaviors, such as lying, silent collusion, or denial, typically found in addiction systems are also found in repressive or abusive systems. Traditional organizations based on command and control operations obsessed with winning at all cost, train and reward people to behave in ways similar to addictive systems. These dysfunctional behaviors occur so frequently in businesses today they are considered "normal" ways of operating. Though these behaviors may be the norm it doesn't mean they are healthy, let alone morally and spiritually valid.

Unfortunately, because these behaviors are considered normal, they are not questioned. However, for greater healing and spiritual growth, we must critically examine these behaviors. As we gain more clarity and become more intentional about what we do, we begin to see there are other options for behaving. Spiritual practice allows people the opportunity to be intentional and make informed choices for action based on greater guidance and inner strength.

Addicts, like repressive authority figures, don't treat others with respect, consideration, and understanding. They set up conditions in which the addiction, like repression, can be maintained. In this way, addictive or repressive environments are antithetical to spiritually nurturing environments. They prevent people from finding and living their wholeness.

In a study done by the Hazelden Foundation, the researchers found that a vast majority of people (86%) would be comfortable talking to a co-worker about drug and alcohol abuse, but only 20% had actually done so. The costs of ignoring addiction problems in the workplace are enormous, but there are steps that organizations can take in addressing substance abuse. Several steps suggested by Human Resource experts include having a clear policy on substance abuse, establishing and publicizing EAP support, and teaching employees how to intervene and how to deal with failed interventions.[2] It is important to create opportunities for people to talk about their addictions so their healing can begin.

A brief review of addiction and addictive systems is necessary to understand how organizations are affected by and perpetuate addictions. In addictive environments, the addict becomes so self-centered and consumed by her addiction, everyone else continually is pulled into her addiction. This imbalance of focus in addictive environments stifles effective human relations. It does not allow confrontation or open communication but instead perpetuates defensive communication patterns such as those describe previously.

Members of addictive systems generally play out one of four roles to handle the unpredictable and painful environment created by the addiction. These roles are:

- Hero or rescuer – person tries to put the broken pieces back together and/or fix the situation

- Scapegoat or martyr – person tries to take the blame so the addict doesn't have to

- Lost child or withdrawn – person withdraws physically or psychologically to avoid the craziness

- Mascot or comic – person uses humor or other tactics to lighten the pain

Greater spiritual practice at an individual or group level will often expose these learned patterns of behavior. As people become more aware of their armor and become more intentional about living spiritually, they see what patterns and roles they have developed. Often, these roles are played out in work groups where some members are the "rescuers," others are the addicts, and others are the "lost children." Still others are the martyrs, scapegoats, mascots, or comics, each dancing the dance learned so well over the years.

One woman I met several years ago described her work for an international advertising agency where cocaine use on the job was normal and even encouraged so that employees could be creative. She questioned this practice, not only on legal grounds but for health considerations, and was scorned by her colleagues. She didn't realize at the time that she was made the scapegoat for questioning the dysfunctional behavior. Eventually she left for a smaller firm with less prestige and pay but regained her spirit and integrity. Here is a vivid case where the organization, through its norms and reward system, acted literally as the addict.

Unfortunately, dishonesty and collusion with dysfunctional practices become normal, acceptable behaviors, and few people feel powerful enough to challenge it. Those who question the dysfunctional behaviors are simply told "that's just how it is around here" as a justification for continuing such behavior. It is often a painful process, pointing out to others the dysfunctional behaviors. To sustain such dysfunction, organizations often punish or repress those who speak out and bring to light such dysfunctional actions.

Many who challenge dysfunctional behaviors find they can no longer stay in such an environment and keep their sanity or integrity. An accountant friend who was fired from such a dysfunctional organization said it was the best thing that could have happened to him. He was looking for a way out and this was the impetus to switch careers.

It's quite common for burnout, turnover, or illness to strike an entire department where the supervisor is a workaholic. Usually in workaholic or other addictive situations, the person with the addiction lacks balance in his life and so creates that imbalance for others. Examples of workaholic behavior include supervisors who call or e-mail employees at home after hours with new demands for work to be done. One client of mine described how her supervisor asked her to carry a beeper on her wedding day in case he needed to reach her! It is important to identify when a supervisor doesn't accept the boundaries of the employees' personal lives. It causes emotional and/or physical stress for those employees who feel they need to jump at every call or fall in line with every demand. I generally point out the unhealthy behaviors as violating the employees' personal boundaries or urge them to honor their personal time to recharge their batteries. It is often very hard for people to see that they have a choice in whether or not to continue playing into the workaholic conditions.

CO-DEPENDENCY

Co-dependent behavior of non-addicts are actions people take that support the addiction. Addicts need the co-dependent person to enable them to keep their addictions. Such enabling includes shielding the addiction from public scrutiny, or providing money to continue the addiction. Co-dependents don't feel they can or should challenge the addict to address her woundedness. Family members learn how to cover for an alcoholic or to take the blame for mistakes to protect the alcoholic so he doesn't have to live with the consequences of the addiction.

It is important that people see the difference between having a *spiritual life of service* and being a co-dependent. Co-dependents derive their importance and sense of self by "fixing" others or doing for the other so the addict doesn't have to be responsible for his actions. Co-dependents often are shut off from healthy ways of living and lose perspective of their needs in their relationship. Their life and the life of the addict are so intertwined that the co-dependent can't find his wholeness without the other person being sick or unbalanced. Co-dependents are blind to the disservice they do to others by their helping. Rather than offering service to others by helping them grow, co-dependents support and perpetuate the unhealthy behaviors.

Too often another's addiction is transparent to the co-dependent because they see their role as helping on behalf of the person they care about. Though not called co-dependency until recent years, this type of dysfunctional behavior was identified as harmful several thousand years ago. In the Bhagavad Gita, the Lord Krishna says, "Do your duty, however imperfectly. To do the duty of another, however perfectly, places you in Great Spiritual Danger."

Do your duty, however imperfectly. To do the duty of another, however perfectly, places you in Great Spiritual Danger.

— Bhagavad Gita

People who live in addictive systems can themselves become addicts or become co-dependents. Many people who work in the "helping professions" such as social service, medicine, or ministry are co-dependents or come from families with addictions.

Adult Children of Alcoholics (ACOAs) play out behaviors and roles learned from their childhood addictive family system. These behaviors and roles are found in most organizations as well. ACOAs tend to exhibit one or more of the following characteristics:

1. Crisis handlers
2. Controlling
3. Workaholic
4. Resistant, defiant
5. Perfectionist, self-critical
6. Loner, isolated

Co-dependents and ACOAs must go through a recovery process to be effective with their clients and co-workers the same way addicts must go through recovery. In the recovery process, co-dependents learn to derive their sense of self-worth on their own achievements, not by supporting another's unhealthy behavior. The path to greatness is one of service to others by recognizing *your own purpose* and using your gifts, rather than feeling your purpose and gifts are unimportant.

WORK AS ADDICTION; ORGANIZATIONS AS ADDICTS

Because organizations are social systems, interpersonal relationships mirror those learned in previous social systems, most notably one's family. Thus, dysfunctional behavior patterns learned in previous addictive systems are often transferred to the workplace. Organizations not only provide the stage in which addiction can be carried out, they also can play the role of the drug dealer supplying the addictive substance, that is work itself.

In their book *The Addictive Organization*, Anne Wilson Schaef and Diane Fassel describe how organizations can be addicts or the addictive substance. Their analysis of workaholism as "the clean addiction," one that is socially sanctioned and encouraged, is enlightening. Through the process of work itself, people avoid pain in their life or lose their sense of self in their work. In this way, work becomes the fix and the employee becomes an addict willing to ignore and damage other aspects of their life in order to sustain their fix. It is important to understand that the "fix" in workaholism is the *activity of working*, not the outcome or product of the work.

Below is a brief outline of the characteristics and behaviors related to addiction and co-dependency.[3]

Addict	Co-dependent
Creates crisis, confusion, and chaos	Server, sufferer
Self-centered (other life activities come second to the addiction)	Protecting (in the guise of caring for) the addict
Dishonest; good con, and liar	Dishonest, in collusion with the addict
Perfectionism; doesn't feel worthy or good enough	Enabler - maintains and perpetuates situations that should fall apart
Controlling/Illusion of Control	Do what is popular rather than right

From the above list of addict characteristics, it is easy to see how an organization can act as an addict. In very unhealthy organizations, work is done in patterns similar to how addicts behave. Work is constantly in a state of confusion or crisis. Perfectionism is the norm of operating, making people feel unworthy or not good enough if they don't achieve an unobtainable level of performance. The organization demands people become so absorbed in the wellbeing of the organization (self-centeredness) that members must give up all other activities on behalf of the organization.

The implications of addictions in and by organizations merit serious consideration. With respect to organizations as addicts, how much annual profit is "good enough?" In a win-at-all-cost business environment, addictive behaviors are usually the norm (perfectionism, illusion of control, workaholism), while ethical behavior and use of conscience is considered disruptive to effective organizational performance. To create spiritually supportive organizations, we must critically examine our economic system that rewards organizational profits regardless of the cost to healthy human relations. How often do investment analysts and industry experts give weight to the human relations within an organization when establishing financial ratings or making financial predictions?

As in co-dependency, an organization's continual external reference to outside sources to define its success (e.g., media pundits, competitors, or institutional investors) diminishes its focus on action that is spiritually-principled. Consumers have a major role to play by purchasing products and making investments in companies whose internal policies and actions promote greater personal wellbeing.

We must be intentional about seeing the roles we play in an addictive system and how our own and others' addictive behavior patterns are perpetuated. Once dysfunctional patterns are brought to awareness, people can be taught other coping behaviors and healthier patterns for interacting. Companies with Employee Assist Programs (EAP) could do more to educate workers about co-dependency behaviors and train staff on ways to help, while not enabling a co-worker who has an addiction problem. People must see they have a *choice* in whether the current patterns are ones they want to continue.

People involved in addiction, whether they are the addict or a co-dependent, usually block out or avoid emotions. People in addictive environments develop patterns of behavior that shut down or block pain caused by the addict. Most of the behavior patterns are learned as coping strategies for the unpredictable, unreasonable, and often crazy environments caused by the addict. However, these behaviors become problems when they are generalized to other situations where there is no addiction. More significantly, these dysfunctional behaviors prevent the addiction from being corrected and prevent the wounds from being healed.

In order for healing to happen at work, organizations must support this process. Organizations must be willing to try an intervention to help groups affected by addiction or other injurious behavior deal with their problems. Group members and organizational leaders must be aware that interpersonal relations and productivity are likely to get worse before they get better. Members must stay committed to working through the long process of healing together.

Why do you see the speck that is in your brother's eye but do not notice the log that is in your own eye? You hypocrite, first take the log out of your own eye and then you will see clearly to take the speck out of your brother's eye.

— Matthew 7:3-6

If a workgroup decides to be intentional about working through an addiction, it doesn't mean they will stop "producing" while they are going through the process. Healing and recovery occurs along side everyday operations. People are more aware of their individual roles and behavior patterns that support unhealthy behavior. As a group, try taking 30 minutes once a week to reflect on how members' behaviors are affecting others. This can help set the tone of support for healing. This type of group processing will make operations go smoother as misperceptions and conflicts are addressed.

When we make a commitment to follow the path to greatness, we will likely encounter past injuries or addictions that need to be healed to move forward. We each have a role to play in creating greater healing and wholeness. You will need to understand your own and others' behavior patterns and feelings, learn how to work with others in addictions, and offer spiritual support for those going through the healing process. By doing so, you will grow spiritually and help others in their journey as well.

EXERCISES

1. Imagine you had one week to spend by yourself (with your basic food and shelter needs attended to). What would bring you joy during that week? Who or what would you miss that might otherwise bring you satisfaction? Does that person or thing support your life's journey to wholeness? Can you sit with yourself and find peace and comfort in the moment?

2. Reflect on those times when you've been most stressed or frustrated. What do you turn to as a source of strength, comfort, or support? Think of someone you respect as living a healthy, fully attuned life. What do they do to deal with stressful situations? If you don't know what they do, ask them for their insights.

3. Think of someone for whom you've felt responsible for their physical or emotional well being. How do you feel when that person falters or is hurt? Can you disconnect your sense of wholeness or self-worth from their success or self-worth?

PART III

WORKING SPIRITUALLY
WITH OTHERS

11

SACRED TRUST

God doesn't give us a task we are not ready to handle. I just wish
sometimes He didn't trust me so much.

— Mother Theresa

INGREDIENTS OF TRUST

Trust is the centerpiece to all human relationships. Trust is built on *being trustworthy*. In order to be trustworthy you must have integrity and maturity (both spiritual/moral maturity and emotional maturity). We must be mindful of and ever present to our values and principles so that they guide our behavior. In this way, we establish ourselves as trustworthy and help build trusting relationships.

We need to live according to the age-old notion that a person's word is his honor.

Unfortunately, too many people have abused that notion of trust for their own gain. There is a saying in business that often runs counter to our cultural norm for trust and fairness. This saying is "nice guys finish last." The implied message is that you have to cheat or not be trustworthy to get ahead, or if you are nice you will be taken advantage of. And if the primary concern is personal self-interest rather than social interest, then this message is true. However, the spiritual path calls you to continually extend your actions from your spiritual foundation.

Another key ingredient to building trust is personal honesty and authenticity. We must speak our truths from our authentic center. Similarly, people must learn and practice being responsible for their actions and own their feelings. Too many people pass blame on to someone else to cover their mistakes. This does little to build trust with others and certainly isn't being responsible for one's actions.

Despite how difficult it may be at times to practice honesty at work, it is an important step along the path for greatness. Organizations also must be intentional about supporting honest practices. One way to build trust in organizations is to have honest accounting and open books (i.e., access to financial records for anyone in the company) so that people will know the true financial condition of the organization. This would go a long way in building trust in times of downsizing and restructuring.

Another essential ingredient to building trust is courage. To be honest and have integrity, you must have courage to do what you believe is principled action. Much more needs to be said about courage in organizations and what prevents people from feeling courageous to act according to their principles. Even when there isn't a trusting environment and despite possible reprisals, spiritually great people act because they have not only integrity but also courage. Where does this courage come from?

People on the path for greatness feel courageous when they have the skills and self-confidence to make change (confidence means "with – faith"). You will have greater courage to act in the face of fear when your spiritual soil is rich and nourished. Courage also comes from a deep conviction in doing the right thing. The bedrock of this conviction and courage then is faith – faith that your actions serve a greater purpose and faith in your moral or spiritual foundation. To make a leap of faith means you have the courage to act even when you don't know the outcome of your actions but know it is something you must do.

Conversely, many people feel discouraged (lacking courage) to act. When employees are not empowered, often they are discouraged. They lack the courage to act because of fear. Their fear may be based on real or perceived retaliation. It is understandable not to put your neck out for doing what you think is right when you have seen a co-worker try to implement a new idea only to get burned for doing so. In order to turn this discouragement around, people need to be encouraged to do what they can in a safe and trusting environment.

Managers frequently fail to see how their actions or the organization's policies, reward systems, or structures dis-courage employees. Some managers spend years tearing down people's power so that the manager can maintain his own power base, or so the manager won't feel threatened. The end-result is that over time, the manager erodes employee courage to take action. It should not be surprising then when that same manager wants people to feel empowered or take responsibility for change, the employees back away from such a request. In these situations, the manager may think the employees are being slackers for not taking initiative without recognizing that his own actions created an environment where the employees are discouraged. Trust has been eroded all along the way.

MAINTAINING TRUST

Trust is crucial not only to interpersonal relations but to whole systems of democracy and commerce. The political apathy and malaise in the U.S. is but one example of the consequence of mistrust of public officials and government not acting in our best interest. Unions were created because of poor work environments and where trust was eroded. Manufacturing organizations today that don't have unions recognize that they must maintain a basic level of trust or else employees will want to organize to get their needs met. Ironically, unions serve as a tool to keep enough trust in "the system" to keep people working, but when unions create too much distrust of management the whole organization suffers.

Business executives must take personal responsibility to be trustworthy and accountable not only to stockholders but also to key stakeholders such as employees and the public. Likewise, employees and citizens must accept responsibility for their part in building trust, not only as watch dogs, but also by their trustworthy actions. Frivolous law suits only tear down trust.

Each one of us must make a commitment to building our integrity, authenticity, and trustworthiness. One leader who showed his greatness is Aaron Feuerstein, CEO of Malden Mills Industries. By demonstrating loyalty and commitment to his employees, Feuerstein maintained valuable trust. Feuerstein gambled his life savings and the future of his company by remaining loyal to his employees when a fire destroyed a textile plant in Massachusetts.[1] The easy decision would have been to close the plant and head south for cheaper labor. Instead Feuerstein told all 3,000 employees they would receive their full pay and benefits for 90 days while they rebuilt the plant. Within two months 70% of the workforce was back on the job, and within two years all employees who wanted to return to work were able to do so. His loyalty and trust in his staff was mirrored back not only by greater loyalty and trust from the staff but also in greater productivity. Before the fire the mill produced 130,000 yards/week; six weeks after the fire the mill's productivity reached over 200,000 yards/week. Annuals sales grew to $400 million within three years.

Feuerstein acted on his convictions and spiritual principles to do the right thing. He believed that taking care of others was as important as earning profits. He understands the Stakeholder approach that emphasizes that multiple constituents are served by the corporation. Feuerstein said at the new plant dedication, "We must show workers the kind of loyalty they extend to us. When companies act in an ethical way, it's good for business and good for the shareholders." He knows that you can't make the best quality product if you don't have respect for the employees making it.

There is no doubt that Fuerstein's efforts not only endeared greater loyalty but also greater trust. Aaron Feuerstein understands the importance of trust. In a talk shortly after the fire, Feuerstein told the audience, "Trust and loyalty can never, never be broken.... I know clearly that when we're all done with all the machinery and all the professional people, in the last analysis, it depends upon the worker on the floor, the blue collar guy. And if he wants you to win, you win that quality battle. And if he wants you to lose, you lose it. Once you break your trust with him, you never can make it up again. There's no way to put it together again." [2]

Feuerstein draws his sense of integrity and ethics from his strong religious upbringing and from the role model of his grandfather who started the company. During a talk about his role in rebuilding his company, Feuerstein felt uncomfortable taking a hero's applause for what he did.[3] He is concerned that in today's business world he is seen as a hero and champion of ethical business practice. In his eyes, he did what any business leader should have done. He feels corporate America needs to merge laws of spirit with laws of business. Feuerstein quotes eloquently from passages that he learned as a child, from Leviticus and Jeremiah, that instruct business owners and land owners on how to be good businessmen and farmers. In these ancient texts are teachings for ethical business and being true to God.

When asked at a presentation if he had any doubts about his decision to rebuild his plant, he said unwaveringly, "No." For two generations his mill has been a family business that is connected to the community. In a pending lawsuit against his company, Feuerstein could stand to lose much. He has chosen to fight the case fully because he feels if he loses the lawsuit, it would be not only a defeat for himself and his company, but for the very principles for which he stands.

As Feuerstein knows, when trust is broken, it is very difficult to build back up. At the summer camp where I was a counselor, we used to tell the following Native American story; it illustrates how delicate trust is.

> Two boys were such good friends growing up they called each other brother. They learned to fish, hunt, and ride horses together. They played every day and eagerly waited for the day they could join the men in hunting trips.
>
> The summer of their 12th year they prepared for a series of tests to determine if they were ready for hunting with the men. One of the boys, Little Arrow, saw his friend, Cloud Dancer, cheat during part of the test by stealing furs which he

said he trapped. Little Arrow was deeply saddened by what Cloud Dancer had done. They both passed the test but their friendship was never the same.

Cloud Dancer tried repeatedly to get their friendship back. He went to Little Arrow and offered to play games and asked to fish together, but Little Arrow only halfheartedly agreed. Everyone in the village noticed that the boys weren't playing together and had grown apart. An elder told Cloud Dancer to speak to the Chief to resolve the problem.

The Chief called the boys to his tent and asked each to tell what he knew. When Little Arrow told what he saw, Cloud Dancer did not deny it. The Chief then asked the boys to get a feather pillow and meet him at the top of the ridge above the village. The boys did as they were instructed and met the Chief on the ridge. The Chief held the feather pillow high above his head, took out his knife and cut a long slit in the pillow. He shook the pillow and the feathers floated in all directions.

"Go now and collect the feathers" the Chief instructed. The boys scurried quickly about trying to get all the feathers. They grabbed what they could around them and ran to the edge of the ridge for more. After a time it dawned on them that other feathers had blown far away and were caught in the tops of trees. They came back to the Chief with disappointed eyes.

"Have you gotten all the feathers?" the Chief asked.

"No, we have not. Some have scattered too far in the wind," replied Little Arrow.

"Some are up in the tree tops and we can't get to them," replied Cloud Dancer.

"Exactly, my sons," replied the Chief "So too is the way of trust between friends. Remember this always so you don't do anything else that will damage the bonds between you. If you cut the bonds and scatter the feathers, you will never be able to put the pillow back together."

People mislead or injure others all in the name of winning (or progress, shareholder interest, etc.). But winning without examining the human costs, such as violating or diminishing trust, will have short-term gains. Eventually the broken trust will come back to cause enormous barriers to getting things done in the future. Too often, achievement is rewarded at the expense of trust.

Unfortunately, too many people get to adulthood learning about trust the hard way. Too many feathers have been scattered for some people to ever feel they can trust again. For these people the lesson of trustworthiness is still important. Indeed, perhaps the most important spiritual practice is to be trustworthy even if you don't feel you can trust others. Your trustworthiness establishes your credibility and integrity. In this way, others will be able to trust you and will likely act in return in more trustworthy ways.

In order for groups to rebuild trust, they must be aware of their personal biases and fear, be open to new information that may help them understand others better, and be willing to change their opinions and judgments of others. Trust can be rebuilt, but it will require healing on the part of those affected by the broken trust.

TURF GUARDING AND SCARCITY
VS. SHARING AND ABUNDANCE

For teams and organizations to build partnerships, they must share in the good times and bad. When the company succeeds, everyone should benefit, when the company falters, everyone must sacrifice. However, too many times people build fiefdoms in organizations, which they then set out to protect. They do not share resources, knowledge, or ideas with others outside their fiefdom for fear it will be used against them. This siege mentality drains energy and ultimately diminishes productivity in organizations. Turf guarding comes out of a scarcity mentality. Through focusing on what one has that can be shared, people build a greater sense of what can be expanded. Fear results in scarcity, Love builds abundance.

A friend shared a story of the impact low trust had on his clients' ability to use his company's products. His company makes software for manufacturers and sends its training staff to help the client companies learn how to use the software. The benefit of this software is that it allows different parts of the factory to combine their data to determine peak and stress loads on the equipment and to prevent injuries. As lead trainer for the software company, my friend lamented that while the technology is there to reduce injuries and related costs to the company, if the client company staff doesn't share their data with each other, the software is useless.

My friend finds too often that there is mistrust in the client companies over how the data will be used. At the core of this mistrust is turf guarding. The client company's staff members don't share data for fear that they will lose power and thus feel threatened by greater shared knowledge. It is the human components of fear, mistrust, personal status and self-interest that prevent the client companies from reducing their costs. Spending thousands of dollars on the software and countless hours in training aren't going to help most of the companies prevent injuries and equipment inefficiencies. It is the human relationships that need to be improved in these companies. Trust is at the core of those problems.

Another typical mistake organizations make is to take resources from one division to build up another without telling all parties involved what the overall purpose is in making such a change. When people don't see the larger purpose of resource reallocation, it inevitably destroys a sense of unity across divisions and often leads to fiefdom hoarding. Stealing from Peter to pay Paul is a risky strategy and should be done judiciously, otherwise in the end everyone loses.

Similarly, when top executives earn 200 to 500 times more than front line staff, abundance is not spread through the organization. Current incentive packages for executives, often not even tied to company performance, emphasize the value only of the top few players, while not recognizing the impact of everyone's contribution to the whole organization. Employee stock ownership is one way to share abundance throughout the company. Without distributing the gains more equitably, these extreme payoffs to CEOs create mistrust and diminish a feeling of collective wellbeing. Organizations must build a sense of teamwork across divisions and levels so that the strands of the web hold strongly throughout the organization.[4] More outrageous is when plants close with hundreds of people out of work and top executives walk away with lucrative bonuses. Companies must do a better job of sharing the wealth when things go well and sharing the pain when things go wrong.

By being trustworthy and living according to your spiritual principles, you will create change for those who have not seen how to do so. When you choose to follow the path for greatness, you need to anticipate being a change agent. You will need courage to act with integrity and honesty when others around you are not doing so. Be mindful of the daily interactions and various ways trust is either built or broken. Make a personal commitment to be trustworthy at all times and ask that others you work with make this commitment as well. In this way, we hold each other up to standards of spiritual greatness.

EXERCISES

To help build trust in your work group try these:

1. Group Discussion – Each person should share their story while the others listen and not comment or ask questions. Good listening also includes not using body language to convey feelings or respond while others are talking.

    a. Each person should think of an episode when they demonstrated their trustworthiness to someone else.

    b. Each person should think of an episode when they had to trust someone else to do something that was important to them and the person proved to be trustworthy.

2. Fishbowl – This is a good exercise to build better understanding between groups that have low trust of one another. It takes about 4 to 5 hours to complete. This is best done with an outside facilitator the first time you try it.

    Use two groups who must agree at the beginning to listen to each other with an openness to hear the other side. Each group writes down three questions or topics they would like to hear the other group discuss or answer.

    Taking turns, one group goes into the center of the "fishbowl" while the other group circles them (as if outside the fishbowl looking in). The group in the center responds to one question from the outer group. The center group is given approximately 20 minutes to discuss *amongst themselves* the question or topic presented.

The outer group simply watches and listens without responding while the inner group talks. It is extremely important that the outer group not use body language or make sounds that will distract the center group from their conversation with each other. The outer group needs to listen with open ears and heart.

Then the groups trade places and the outer group moves into the center and gets 10 minutes to respond amongst themselves to what the other group said. The new outer group should not respond in body language or sounds to distract the center group. After 10 minutes, the outer group gives the center group one of their questions and they have 20 minutes to discuss it in the fishbowl.

Each group should answer the three questions, with the first center group getting their last chance for a 10 minute discussion to how the outer group answered their last question. Then everyone forms a larger circle together. The whole group can discuss what they learned from each other that they hadn't known or understood before. From there the group can agree to meet again or discuss ways that they can build better communication and understanding in the future.

12

Teamwork: Spirit of the Whole

We do not weave the web of life; we are merely a strand in it.
Whatever we do to the web, we do to ourselves.

— Chief Seattle

The web of life is a metaphor that describes our interdependence with one another. Nowhere do we feel that web more keenly than in small groups, such as teams or families. We know that we are directly impacted by the actions of others in these small groups. We are shaped by them, and in return we shape them.

There is a Buddhist web of life metaphor that demonstrates wonderfully how we are a part of one another. A web contains crisscrossed strands that are connected at juncture points. In each juncture point there is a different diamond representing each one of us. A diamond reflects out light and the images that come into it. In this way, our individual light, our essence, reflects back all the others on the web. Thus, the web of life is filled with hundreds and thousands of diamonds, each sparkling and reflecting outward, while at the same time taking in light from all the other diamonds.

When we see ourselves and each other as these sparks of light and see that our individual light contains each other's light, we understand our interdependence. Or to use a phrase of Thich Naht Hanh's, "we enhance our Interbeing." It is then our quest to not only make our light brighter, but to help the light of others shine bright as well. In this way, teamwork can be a powerful tool for organizational productivity and personal growth.

The web metaphor is helpful for seeing how teams work. We all have gifts that we can share, our unique reflection of light, whether it is in our knowledge, our experiences, our humor, our interpersonal skills, etc. Teams that function best know when to use the various gifts available in the group and help each other grow in areas where members aren't strong. Many MBA programs use study groups with members assigned to teams based on diverse skills and experience. Effective study groups learn to draw from each other's strengths and help different members learn those areas where they are weaker.

Just as a choir or sports team must blend their talents together to a unified whole, so too must work groups strive to become cohesive and flow with one another. This takes not only conscious effort to coordinate skills and talents, but it takes commitment and discipline to sustain a team. It requires being intentional about feeding the collective whole.

How much time and training is spent on learning and intentionally practicing interpersonal and team skills in your organization? How much time is wasted because there aren't good team skills and processes in your organization? It never ceases to amaze me that we assume people know how to work together even though much of our lives have been spent in educational institutions that value individual achievement over group accomplishment.

The more our school systems are forced to cut extracurricular activities where teamwork is essential, such as band, theater or student clubs, the less likely children will learn interpersonal and social skills for effective group process. Many schools don't have gym class or recess anymore. Yet these are missed opportunities to teach sportsmanship, conflict resolution skills, cooperation, and other important interpersonal skills.

Unfortunately, we can't assume children will learn these at home or in religious institutions. The burden will be on businesses of tomorrow to teach these interpersonal and team skills since we can't assume people will have these along with other basic job skills. Businesses need to examine whether they include team skills as part of their performance appraisal process. As teams are used more in organizations, job performance will need to be evaluated for effective interpersonal skills as much as technical skills and meeting job-specific goals. In addition, team success needs to be recognized or rewarded more so than individual success if teamwork is to be seen as valuable in an organization.

The following story is of one of my favorite summer camp chapel stories.

Angels in Training

A man was sent to heaven and given a tour of the training facilities. His tour guide first showed him a room where the angels-in-training were getting ready to have breakfast. The angels-in-training sat across from one another down a long table. Placed before each angel-in-training was a bowl of cereal, some milk, and a 6 foot long wooden spoon.

At the sound of a chime, the angels-in-training began eating their breakfast. Because the spoon was so long, the angels-in-training had difficulty feeding themselves. Cereal flew around the room and milk splattered everywhere. At the end of breakfast everyone grumbled and complained about going hungry.

The tour guide then took the man to the room where the angels had their breakfast. This room was set up exactly the same, with a long table, seats facing each other, bowls of cereal and milk, long wooden spoons. However, the angels looked perfectly happy with their breakfast. In fact, the room was spotless, no stray cereal or splatter of milk.

The man was a bit confused by the sight. He turned to his guide and said, "Did the angels have the same thing to eat as the angels-in-training?" "Yes," replied the guide. "Do you want to know why the angels aren't hungry?" "Of course" replied the man. "Because the angels know that if they feed the person across from them they will be fed. In this way, serving another is the way to fulfillment. Serving yourself only leaves you hungry."

TEAMWORK WITH DIFFICULT PEOPLE (A.K.A., ANGELS-IN-TRAINING)

Various management consultants have outlined key ingredients for creating high performance teams.[1] Most of these ideas are based on the assumption that people have good interpersonal skills so that people really listen to one another and ideas are presented effectively. They also assume that team members can treat one another with respect. However, these essential ingredients are not always present. Too frequently, team members have developed a history of antagonism towards each other, they don't trust one another, or they push each other's hot buttons. Indeed, current books and ideas on dealing with really difficult people argue that some certain percentage of people simply don't try to get along because they are more interested in power and control than working cooperatively with others.[2] What do you do when team members can't stand to be with one another, let alone work as a group? How do you work with others who get under your skin or who refuse to cooperate?

Rather than define difficult team members as "jerks" or people who should be avoided whenever possible, I suggest coming up with ways to interact with them as Divine Holy Beings (angels-in-training) even if what they do is anything but Divine or Holy. Many faith traditions hold the tenet that we all carry a spark of the Divine within us. When we view others as Divine Beings we immediately reframe how we think of people.

We have all been given the same mission as spiritual beings, which is to navigate successfully through life and do our best at any given moment. This sometimes seems the hardest to do at work. So, when someone is having a hard time at work, and is perhaps making life hard for those around them, remember that they are on the same journey as you.

Many times, really difficult people don't view themselves as worthwhile human beings and so treat everyone else as inferior people not worthy of respect or caring. These difficult people have usually learned that to survive in the world they must compete and control others lest they be hurt, either physically or emotionally.

When you treat really difficult people as spiritual beings, you affirm their worthiness and accept them for who they are. By your spiritually loving response, you show them they don't need to control or be hurtful to work with you. This takes an incredible amount of empathy, compassion, and respect on your part. However I have found it is better to offer Divine Love rather than lash back with anger or hurtful comments. Reacting from your pain often only leads to greater antagonism and adds fuel to the fire. Treating others as spiritual beings is a more constructive approach than writing them off as people you can't work with and possibly adding hostility to the already tense group dynamics. Use your inner strength to be gentle not judgmental. This will take practice because it is not easy to refrain from judgments in tense situations.

At the same time, it is essential we look within ourselves to determine why our hot buttons are triggered so easily. As Eleanor Roosevelt once said, "No one can make you feel inferior unless you let them." Your inward focus can be done with some of the spiritual techniques outlined in earlier chapters, or you may need professional assistance from a therapist or pastoral counselor.

When we recognize we are all One, we understand that others' actions and ours are interlinked and interchangeable. Another's fear is our own. Another's strength is our own.

According to various traditions, other people serve as a mirror to us. We draw those people to us who are not only teachers and instruments for our growth, but who also show us a piece of ourselves as well. Sometimes a harmful action by others serves as a wake-up call for us to examine what actions we also take that are injurious. When we get angry at others for being cruel, judgmental, or rude, we need to stop and ask ourselves "how can I be less cruel or judgmental?" We see in others those same aspects of ourselves. Similarly when we admire others we need to look within to find our own talents and gifts that are admirable. We can become our own heroes.

When we recognize we are all One, we understand that others' actions and ours are interlinked and interchangeable. Another's fear is our own. Another's strength is our own. When we act with compassion instead of anger, we add more compassion to the world.

When our anger is directed towards others who mirror our thoughts or actions, we are angry at ourselves as well. If we are to respond compassionately, we must release our anger by letting go of judgments and forgiving ourselves. Jesus' reprimand "Let he who has not sinned cast the first stone" reminds us that we all have made mistakes and acted in poor judgment. We can not judge others lest we judge ourselves as well.

TAKING RESPONSIBILITY

In a recent consultation, I led an exercise where the staff envisioned what they wanted their department to look like a year later and what their role could be in making that vision a reality. We synthesized and summarized everyone's comments, then discussed what actions seemed reasonable to undertake. One member of the group commented, "What we're talking about here is the Golden Rule." Everyone agreed that if the Golden Rule was followed the department would be a lot better place to work.

Another employee chimed in, "I don't have any trouble applying the Golden Rule, I get along well with everyone I work with." I asked him if that applied to the manager of the department as well. The employee looked concerned at my question and understood the gravity of it. Most of the staff at the meeting were angry with the manager because of actions he had taken that undermined their efforts. I told the employee, "If you want the manager to apply the Golden Rule to everyone, you need to as well. Can you treat him as you would like him to treat you?" The employee was stumped. He really didn't know if he could do it.

This employee believed the Golden Rule should be followed and it was needed particularly at his workplace. Yet when pushed to making a commitment to act towards his manager as he wanted to be treated, which was with respect, kindness, and understanding, he had a hard time swallowing the medicine.

The Golden Rule is simple to grasp yet so difficult to apply. Why is that? Because people often want others to treat them *differently* than they are willing to treat others. If you want others to treat you with respect, you must do so in return or better yet, model how that behavior looks even if others don't act that way towards you.

In the group described above, I ended the meeting telling them that they knew what steps they could take to turn around the department. The question was whether they wanted to start acting differently themselves or did they want to be miserable at work waiting for the manager to change. The key for them was to start where they were and take responsibility for their actions.

It often takes only a few people to change how they behave for the morale and mood of a whole department to change. When workers look to their boss for the change, they often wait impatiently and get angry, which only leads to more frustration or escalates a hostile environment. We must take personal responsibility for our actions and life circumstances in order to change our relationships.

Look honestly and deeply at what you do to feed into problems at work. Determine what you can change to shift the energy of your work relationships. In the situation described above, too many of the staff took satisfaction in complaining about the workplace. They even admitted to wasting hours grumbling at how bad things were. They knew it only made matters worse, because they not only fed the frustration and air of despair at work, but they got behind in their work and had to stay late to finish it all.

Taking personal responsibility is sometimes the most difficult first step to take. If you play the "Ain't it Awful Game," the first step you must take is to stop wasting time playing this game that feeds the fire of hopelessness. Take responsibility for comments you make that are hurtful, for silence that serves as aggression, for selective memory that makes others' work more difficult, for not listening to others. These are just a few examples of the dozens of actions that go unnoticed in every office every day that block good human relations. Be aware of your actions, thoughts, words, and intentions that don't serve the greater good.

Take ownership of your failings and take responsibility for correcting them. Positive self talk helps to correct actions without beating yourself up. A management consultant I know teaches people to say to themselves: "That is not like me to (name the mistake). Next time I will (name the solution)." This kind of positive coaching is a powerful way to recognize when you have made a mistake, and affirms that you are and can do better.

Namaste:

I salute that place in you wherein resides the center of the Universe.

I salute that place in you wherein resides truth and love and peace and beauty.

I salute that place in you where when you are in that place in you and I am in that place in me we are One.

There is a word that I really like to use and find especially useful for greeting people with whom I feel resentment or frustration. This greeting is "Namaste." One meaning of Namaste is "That which is Holy in me, greets that which is Holy in you." I try to remember this phrase when I work with someone who triggers my hot buttons. This word helps me to remember the other person is also a Divine being. Think of how differently you would feel about an annoying person in your work group if every time you saw that person, you greeted them with this phrase and thought to yourself, "here stands a Holy person in front of me." You will connect with this person on a deeper, spiritual level.

PARTNERSHIP VS. SUPERIORITY

Many people have what Rudolf Dreikurs calls a "teeter-totter" worldview. As in a teeter-totter, one person can be up only by pushing the other person down. Thus superiority comes only by making someone else inferior. This teeter-totter game is played out emotionally, mentally, physically in countless situations everyday. Unfortunately most people grew up with this way of relating to others and have not learned another way to get along with people. It's better to remember the words of one sage, "If I blow out your candle that doesn't make mine any brighter."

There is nothing noble in being superior to other men. The true nobility is in being superior to our previous self.

— Hindu proverb

To get out of the teeter-totter game, people must see their interdependence with one another. We are not superior or inferior to one another, but interdependent with one another. Unlike the teeter-totter, if one person is pushed down, we are all brought down. As the Indian poet Rabindranath Tagore said, "No civilized society can thrive upon victims...those whom we keep down inevitably drag us down."

Thus, people must not see themselves as a victim of or superior to others, but as partners with others. We are connected strands on a web, not living on teeter-totters. We can not build ourselves up by tearing others down. We must lift people up if we are to feel lifted up. There is a Hindu proverb that says "There is nothing noble in being superior to other men. The true nobility is in being superior to our previous self." In order for people to give their best, they must feel secure and supported. Therefore, effective teams encourage members to help each other feel connected to and supported by each other.

Relationships vs. Heirarchy

Status and hierarchy must be eliminated in order to work as a team. Some people cling to hierarchies because they want authority figures. It is sometimes easier when someone else tells us what to do so we don't have to think for ourselves or be responsible for our actions or decisions. Efforts to create self-directed teams work only to the extent that people can put aside their need for hierarchy.

People must shift from reliance on authority from above to authority from within if they are going to function well as teams. Many people look to others for making decisions, for making things happen, or for permission to try out new ideas. Making the shift from hierarchy and external authority to inner authority is essential for team-based decisions. People must find their power within themselves and with others rather than look for power over others or from others. For effective teams, people must develop their own inner authority to determine their actions.

Organizational members must shift away from hierarchy and let go of the patriarchal mind set where managers are seen as parental figures who hold authority so that others don't have to think. This may be one of the biggest challenges to truly making teams work in organizations.

SPIRITUALLY-GROUNDED GROUP
DECISION-MAKING

There is an expression that "a camel is the result of a committee trying to design a horse." Many of us have walked away from committee meetings frustrated and bewildered at the decisions made. In many cases compromise is required in group work. However, groups don't necessarily have to end up with work that is substandard.

Quaker-style consensus decision-making is based on the belief that there is a group truth beyond the individual truths. I use the phrase "building the Spirit of the Whole" to describe this group process. This style of decision making goes beyond using a decision-making rule, like strong or weak majority rule, but uses a spiritual process for understanding the unfolding truths of a group. To arrive at decisions in this way involves less talking and analysis. It involves silent reflection not just on the facts presented, but on searching deep within to discern the collective truth. Coming to consensus in this way involves finding a solution or decision that everyone can live with, and one that feels like a deeply rooted decision.

Quakers believe that we each have a piece of the Divine Truth. Perhaps more importantly Quakers recognize that others also reveal the Divine and no individual has the whole Divine Truth. It is by sharing our personal truths with the truth of others that we can know a greater truth.

Spiritual decision-making builds on this process of discovering our Divine truth. It goes past personal egos or having a specific person's idea adopted. Spiritual decision-making is based on discovering a Higher Wisdom that is better than any individual's view. Discernment in a group is time consuming. Coming to decisions this way takes time and often struggle. It is often difficult to set aside your ego and listen beneath all your mind's chatter to hear the still small voice within. It is a personal struggle to determine what spirit calls us to do rather than what our self-serving desires or other's interests demand us to do.

One way to be open to this Higher Wisdom is to take time during a meeting or discussion to be silent. During this time, remain open to seeing how another's view may be valid or build on what others have said. Don't silently rehearse your position or rationalize why your view is right. Use the silence for reflection and openness to new ideas or insights to emerge. The point of silent meditation like this is to listen for the wisdom of a deeper truth. It takes skill and practice to find this wisdom.

> *Rather than feel that you must "Stand up for Truth if it is ridiculed," just let the Truth in you stand for itself.*
>
> – Myrtle Filmore

Decisions grounded in seeking the highest truth directs our attention and energy to greater levels of thinking and action. In this way, the team can find better solutions as well as build the Spirit of the Whole. Make a commitment to act consistently with a greater truth as it reveals itself to you and your work group.

Multiply the individual struggle of finding our own personal truths by all the others in a group and you can see that spiritual decision making is difficult work. But once it is accomplished, the group has learned how to find the "Spirit of the Whole." Each time the group can tap into the spirit of the whole, the group truth becomes easier to find. When further decisions or actions need to be taken, group members know what they need to do to find their solutions.

One Quaker school principal described how quickly students come to group decisions once they've learned and practiced these techniques. By the time they reach high school, students easily are able to discover their group truths and understand what needs to be done. Most importantly, they do it themselves with little intervention from their teachers. This is the ultimate in self-directed teams.

There is a stronger feeling of trust and cohesion that results when teams make decisions this way. Greater understanding comes from finding your own and another person's truth. Groups that reach the "spirit of the whole" develop a sense of "we-ness" rather than just being a collection of individuals. The members' ideas are transformed into group consciousness that become a new entity distinct from the individual views. Not only are decisions better made, but the group feels a strong bond that is useful later to carry out the decision.

As people learn how to find their group consciousness and group truth, they can expand that to more macro levels by searching for the "spirit of the whole" in the organization. There must be a sense of all members working towards the same ends for people to feel committed and connected to the whole organization. The schisms found in many organizations between management and line staff are a result of all parties not seeing themselves as mutually connected to one another. Many spiritual traditions speak of the unity of all creation, that we are all One. We must learn to see the interdependence of all people in our organizations, our nation and our planet. It is a difficult task but one that must be done to achieve the ultimate "Spirit of the Whole."

I'm a big believer in networking, not only connecting people with one another, but also sharing information. On many occasions I have found some information and in conversation shortly thereafter I found the person who needed what I had read or heard. When you pass information on to a team member, it could just be the piece that leads to a break-through. Giving information freely to others is essential to spiritually guided decision making. As the angel story tells us, it is in feeding others that we are fed. Too many times teams go hungry because of turf guarding and other forms of hoarding. Several exercises at the end of this chapter will help you see how to work spiritually in a group setting, either at your work or with friends.

How does a group truth emerge? As discussed earlier in this book you can discern your inner truths through such activities as journal writing, meditation, prayer. You can also use a talking stick or other focusing tool to allow people to speak their truth and listen to the truth of others. When we each share pieces of the truth as we know it, we slowly build the bigger picture, like adding pieces of a jigsaw puzzle. We begin to see things more clearly and get the bigger picture as we contribute what we know and speak our truth.

Now there are varieties of gifts, but the same Spirit; and there are varieties of services, but the same Lord; and there are varieties of activities, but it is the same God who inspires them all in everyone.

To each is given the manifestation of Spirit for the common good.

– I Corinthians 12:4-7

It is an ongoing process to peel off the various layers of learned, prescribed messages imposed from others to be clear on what our own truth is. People must be willing to look at their assumptions of how they work with others and what they expect of others. This process can be very frightening for some people, because it often forces them to question the very core of their being. Most people have adopted truths over the years from institutions, family, and friends without assessing whether their truths and beliefs are useful or still hold. Critically examining one's personal beliefs can be very frightening. At the very least it is uncomfortable.

Going deeper to determine our personal truths is a spiritual process. It often involves letting go of tightly held beliefs or familiar patterns of behavior. Most people resist personal change precisely because it requires letting go of the familiar for the unknown. It requires trust in a larger purpose or process to make oneself vulnerable. It takes a leap of faith. To do this in a work group is extremely difficult unless there is enormous trust and safety with group members. Most groups are not able to do this without an outside facilitator to create safe space and guide the group through the process. With practice and commitment to the process, teams can create their own safe space, and speak their individual and collective truths.

When we see each other as divine beings, seek the truth of the group, and take responsibility for our actions, our work flows smoother. We can bring spirituality to our groups and work teams in such a way that better decisions are made and we grow from the experience. The path to greatness will include working with others. We must learn to bring spirituality to groups and work spiritually as a collective. By doing so, everyone is elevated to a higher level of being.

EXERCISES

(These can be done in retreats or with outside facilitators as half-day workshops.)

1. Each team member writes down their answer to the following questions. They then share their responses to these questions by going around the circle or as people feel inclined to speak. People always have a right to pass and they can't comment on what other people say. This is a time for listening and reflecting, not discussion or debate.

   a. What is one area of your job that you feel you do best?

   b. What is one area of your job that you feel you need help to improve?

   c. What is one thing someone can do that really upsets you (a pet peeve or a hot button)?

   d. What is one aspect of yourself that you really want to change?

   Process:

   a. Once everyone has a chance to share their answers, the group can reflect on common themes or areas of differences that need further attention. People will need to remember to use "I" statements in these discussions.

   b. An alternative to the above group dialogue process is to start with one person who answers these questions then calls the name of another group member to go next. The next person must summarize what the preceding person said before she can speak. When the second person is done, she calls the name of a third person who must summarize what was just said before speaking, etc. This ensures people listen actively to each speaker since they don't know when they will be called.

2. Affirmation Circle –

Process:

a. Have one person sit in the middle of a circle and have the rest of the group spend one minute telling that person the positive qualities he/she posesses. People can speak in any order or simultaneously. Each person has an opportunity to sit in the middle. The time limit for the affirmations is one minute for everyone.

    People must think of personal traits or behaviors that others have and recognize the gifts that others can contribute to the group.

b. (You'll need sticky notes for this option.)

    To do this exercise a little more anonymously, place enough clean sheets of paper on a table so that there is one sheet for each group member. Write the name of a different group member at the top of each sheet. Everyone now writes one affirmation per sticky note for each group member. When the group has finished writing their affirmations, they then place their affirmation sticky notes on each member's piece of paper. After all affirmations are placed on the table, allow time for each person to read the affirmations on his/her own sheet of paper.

Some people feel uncomfortable receiving and giving compliments so this process option may be used. However, it is more powerful to hear the affirmations verbally and directly from others.

3. Areas for growth

    Similar exercise to affirmation circle but have people hear feedback on their areas for personal growth from other members of the group. This feedback should be done in a constructive manner without blame or anger. People may not want to say this directly so the second option may be preferred.

For both exercise 2 & 3, the group may want to process the feedback as a group, noting the common or different themes of areas where people are strong or need more work.

13

SEXUALITY AND SPIRITUALITY

*It is only with the heart that one can see rightly; what is
essential is invisible to the eye.*

– Antoine de Saint-Exupèry, *The Little Prince*

UNDERSTANDING FEAR AND LOVE

There are two roots to human emotions – Fear and Love.
Most people think that the opposite of love is hatred.
But this is not so. The root of hatred comes in fear that someone
will somehow hurt you. If the other cannot hurt you in some
way (physically, emotionally, spiritually, mentally), there is no
reason to hate them. A basic teaching from *A Course in Miracles*
is: "Nothing real can be threatened. Nothing unreal exists.
Herein lies the peace of God."

Let us examine the two roots of human emotion in more depth. It is not always the case that positive emotions are rooted in love and negative emotions are rooted in fear. Often it is just the opposite. It can be that precisely because we are fearful, we fall in love with another so he will protect us from what we fear. Many people fear being alone and thus want to have a relationship so that they will be protected from feeling lonely. People also fear being without food or shelter and thus develop a relationship with someone who will provide these securities for them. They say they love the person when the root of their love is fear.

This holds true for people who look for protection from supervisors or co-workers. People may say they like their boss or their job, when in reality they fear looking for a new job or working for someone else who won't protect them. Many interpersonal relationships that appear to be good ones are unhealthy because they need fear to maintain them. These types of relationships function only so long as the fear remains. When one person grows a stronger sense of herself or no longer fears what she did before, the glue of the relationship comes undone. Ending such a relationship may be the healthiest thing to do for both people.

Conversely, when we deeply love an institution or principle, we will fight, sometimes violently, to defend or support it. Most people have not learned how to stand up for a cause or idea they strongly support in a loving way. Spiritual leaders in our time such as Gandhi, M.L. King, Jr., and the Dalai Lama have modeled how one can fight for something important with Love and win your cause nonviolently. Sadly, because so few of us have experience or training in how to fight for something in Love, it is still a rare occurrence. Too many fights are ego-involved, based on power, greed, or control.

EXPRESSING EMOTIONS AT WORK

Emotions are a natural part of being human. We need to accept rather than deny emotions exist, and to work with our emotions effectively. Emotions will come up at work just as they do at home, however most adults have figured out ways to mask their emotions at work. This masking may be appropriate if people need a cooling-off period, but often people feel it's safer or more comfortable to not deal with the issue that evoked the emotion in the first place. This is a conflict-avoidance style which is ultimately unproductive.

Emotions are acceptable at work because they are what make us human. We can't be fully present at work and fully contribute to work if we deny parts of our humanness. That is not to say that we *always* have to express our emotions at the drop of a hat. Sometimes a time-out for cooling off or talking with a trusted confidant outside the situation is the best approach before acting on those emotions. Emotions need to be channeled constructively rather than shut off or stuffed inside and not addressed.

It is often difficult to express emotions at work in constructive ways. A common maxim that prevents dialogue and conflict resolution is: "If you can't say something nice then don't say anything at all." People who have learned this message never confront others when they need to. They have a hard time dealing with negative emotions such as anger and frustration. Some people shut down emotionally when they are yelled at or rejected.

Others fear expressing their anger because they are afraid of what they will do or say as it all tumbles out. Yet, this pent up anger ultimately will burst forth, whether it is through self-defeating behaviors like addictions, or in illnesses or violent behaviors. People need to find constructive outlets for their anger. Some simple techniques for releasing anger is to write a letter to someone who has harmed you. Release the intensity and hurt through your words. You can decide later to give them the letter or to shred it or burn it. Another approach is to use a picture or symbolic representation of the person or thing that angered you and put it on to a chair in a room by yourself. Vent your anger at that representation allowing yourself to release your anger in whatever form it takes. After you release your anger, offer a healing prayer to yourself and to the other that you may grow to greater wholeness and love. You may have to do these exercises and others many times before you will be fully released from the anger. Find a way to express your emotions in supportive and constructive ways.

SEXUALITY AND SPIRITUALITY

Many people aren't in touch with their emotions because they've learned as children that emotions are bad or are not to be trusted. Even expressing positive emotions at work can lead to misunderstandings if others attribute it to sexual expression. Saying complimentary things can be misconstrued as sexual harassment. It is important to recognize times when our emotions are raised and our passions aroused. Those times when we are inspired and energized by others, while often desirable, sometimes can be confusing or even unhealthy.

Sexuality is powerful energy and if left uncontrolled or misunderstood it can wreak havoc on those involved. To reach the highest form of Love we must learn how to manage sexual energy. The best way to deal with sexuality in the workplace is to examine it fully for what it is rather than leave it unexamined and hope it goes away. We must learn to understand and work with our feelings, and to be intentional about our desires rather than feel victims of them. The power of being human is that we are able to choose how we want to use our emotions.

People are naturally drawn to others who are more loving, compassionate, and understanding. However, it is easy to get confused between romantic attractions or crushes and the Divine Love that comes through us. Spiritual practice and growth tends to increase sexual attractions. People may become more attracted to you, or you may be drawn towards certain people because you or they are on a spiritual path. Being mindful and intentional about our spiritual practice requires that we are careful and aware of our increased spiritual energy and how it can be interpreted as sexual energy.

People need to examine carefully the source of the sexual energy. Many times our sexual desires really have nothing to do with wanting a relationship. People may be bored and want variety, or may want to prove something to themselves or others, or they are risk-takers and want to push the envelope. People can be attracted to others for their power, prestige, fortune, or spirituality. The underlying reason for the attraction or sexual desire must be understood clearly for what it is. Careful reflection and discernment can bring about this clarity.

To help discern what the basis of your feelings are when you feel attracted to another person, a minister friend offered the following guidance. If you feel significantly drawn to another at work, ask yourself – "is your desire for this person a calling or a distraction from something or someone else?" Give yourself plenty of time to reflect on your feelings and carefully review what is producing them. Don't act on such feelings until you've allowed sufficient time to discern why the feelings are emerging and you've determined what action you can take that is spiritually responsible. Be clear on your motives and the consequences of any action you take.

The key to understanding sexuality with respect to spiritual work is that sexual arousal is often confused with increased spiritual energy. In the Chinese tradition we all have Chi, energy that is our life force and runs through us. People who do Tai Chi and Qi Gung feel this energy build through practice. When intensified, this life force or Chi energy can be mistaken for what Freud called libido, sexual energy.

It is important to understand Divine Love as a form of energy exchanged between people.

Research in social psychology has shown that if someone feels their heart rate increase in the presence of an attractive person, they most likely believe the attractive person is the cause of these feelings rather than searching for other causes for these feelings. They increase their liking for the other and label their feelings as being "sexually aroused," even if their heart rate is elevated by environmental causes. Thus, people frequently misattribute the source of their arousal.

Similarly, when people feel increased energy in the presence of a spiritually developed individual, they will misattribute the spiritual form of energy. However, this form of energy is very different from sexual energy. It is Divine Love. It is important to understand Divine Love as a form of energy exchanged between people. When people experience Divine Love from someone, they often think of it as romantic attraction or sexual arousal because they lack another label to give to this different form of energy.

Because we are limited in our understanding and experience in love and the many manifestations of it, Divine Love is often misattributed as romantic love or sexual arousal. Divine Love is unconditional love and doesn't require a loving response in exchange. Unconditional love is unfamiliar to most people since the primary experience of love from family or partners is fairly conditional.

As people become more spiritually developed, they reflect greater Divine Love. They also will receive more such energy. People who live intentionally spiritually are more open to receiving the Divine Love present in all people, and thus may feel attracted to others more easily. Conversely, people generating greater Divine Love will attract others to them. Spiritually-connected people must be very careful how they send out their energy and be clear with people that it can be mistaken for sexual attraction. People who can generate greater Divine Love must be careful how they use their power. Ministers and spiritual teachers know this well.

People who are more spiritually developed will *seem* more sexually charged to others only because sexual arousal (or lust or desire) is the most familiar emotion that we know to identify with this greater energy. As we grow spiritually through work, we must get better at discerning our own and others' increased energy and attribute its source accurately. Spiritual energy needs to be recognized as such and appropriately channeled so it doesn't interfere with or confuse people's lives. I would be remiss in discussing spirituality at work without raising people's awareness of how easy it is to misinterpret increased spiritual energy as sexual attraction.

That's not to say that all feelings of sexual arousal are spiritually based. The point is that feelings identified as sexual energy need to be carefully examined. In work situations it is important to look deeper into your own motives and desires to be clear on why you may feel an attraction to another. It is important to be aware of the various types of energy that feels like sexual arousal and be prepared to discern whether the greater energy is Divine Love, Chi Energy, or some other form.

And Now a Word about Sexual Harassment

Sexual harassment is an important topic in today's work world. Organizations have taken steps to avoid sexual harassment to help their employees work in a safe environment, to minimize the costs of lawsuits, and to avoid bad publicity generated from charges of sexual harassment. Many organizations have sexual harassment policies, procedures, and training to protect members from unwanted sexual advances or hostile work environments.

It is important to recognize that people who sexually harass others often do so for the power and control they have over others rather than for physical pleasure per se. They want to intimidate or control others by their harassing behaviors. Sexual harassment is more often an issue of power than sexual desires.

People undergoing increased spiritual energy must likewise be careful not to misuse their increased energy as power over others. Increased spiritual energy involves becoming an instrument for Divine Love. Using power to diminish another's power by making them feel intimidated or dominated is antithetical to the path of spiritual growth. Spirituality must be used with the primary intention of providing support to others in their growth towards wholeness.

Having said that, I must recognize the fact that some people may misuse their spiritual power in organizations. Clergy have misused their power and their positions as spiritual leaders throughout history. Such misuse is likely to continue, unfortunately, since even spiritually-attuned individuals can falter and resort to unhealthy patterns of behavior. They must attend to their healing as well to follow their growth towards wholeness.

People working with spiritually charged individuals must be mindful of how they feel in the presence of such individuals. If you feel your power diminished or controlled then be cautious of how the other is using her power and critically examine whether she is using this power for your Highest good.

It should be apparent by now that emotions in general, and sexuality in particular, must be acknowledged rather than ignored in your work situations. Through greater spiritual practice and awareness these issues will emerge, sometimes not too subtly. Thus, you need to be aware of them and be prepared to deal with them. Through greater understanding and knowledge of the root causes of these issues, you and your co-workers can work through challenging situations. Quite likely, professional therapists, mentors, or spiritual facilitators will be needed. It will take commitment and energy on the part of everyone involved to support such work.

The best and most beautiful things in the world cannot be seen or even touched. They must be felt with the heart.

– Helen Keller

What is essential is that you and others at your work recognize the dynamics that are created when people grow spiritually. Be aware that sexual energy will be magnified in high energy spiritual environments. All members in your organization must be willing to address when sexual energy occurs rather than avoid it and wish it wouldn't cause problems. People must recognize and deal with sexuality in thoughtful, healthy ways as they follow their path for spiritual greatness.

EXERCISES

1. Think of a time when you were drawn to someone else. What specific characteristics did this person have? Did these characteristics fulfill a need or shortcoming you had in your life? How do these attributes relate to your spirituality or desire to be a more whole and loving person?

2. Imagine yourself being the person you most desire. What characteristics would you change within yourself to be more like this person?

14

ANGER AND RECONCILIATION

I want to know if you can live with failure
yours and mine
and still stand on the edge of the lake
and shout to the silver of the full moon,
"Yes!"

– Oriah House, *The Invitation*

RETRIEVING THE GIFT FROM YOUR ANGER AND FEARS

In the poem, "The Invitation," Oriah House describes the process of being authentic with another, embracing one's pain and sorrow as well as celebrating the ecstasy of life. This poem is such a powerful statement about being completely

196

(whole-ly and holy) present to one another. It is a call to stand before the fire and not shrink back. It requires incredible courage to face your own fears and that of another. Through that process we truly live and grow.

Much has been written about the hero's journey into the darkness. The would-be hero must enter the cave, the underworld, the dark forest, to face his fears. He usually carries with him wisdom in some form that enables him to slay the dragon. Most often this wisdom comes from a teacher or guide. If the hero forgets this wisdom or doesn't use it well, he is defeated.

The success of the Star Wars series comes from re-igniting for a new generation an interest in the hero's journey. This story line goes back centuries as an important part of the initiation to greater wisdom. Sidhartha left his comfortable and safe home to live as an ascetic before he reemerged as the Buddha. Jesus walked in the desert to face his temptations. Later he had to face his death and went into a cave before his rebirth.

Facing one's fears is a powerful process for gaining maturity. Throughout time societies have had rituals for youth to be accepted as adults. These rituals often involved facing one's fears with wisdom and strength. Various Native American tribes used the vision quest to transition into adulthood, with a ceremony to welcome the youth back into the tribe. During these ceremonies, the initiate was often given a new name to recognize the transformation that occurred.

The story of going into the cave or deep forest is powerful because we have all had times when we have had to face our own fears. Some of our most defining moments come when we have to stand up to peer pressure or an authority figure and claim who we are, facing the fear of their rejection or disapproval. The roar of the beast, real or perceived, can be intimidating indeed. David Whyte's book, *The Heart Aroused*, includes wonderful examples of facing our fears in corporate life. He uses myth and metaphor to draw the parallels between the hero's journey and daily corporate episodes when we grab the magical sword or run from the beast.

But the threats and fears don't just come from outside of us. Our own fears and anger can be a powerful beast to wrestle. Many people build thick walls to protect themselves from this beast, keeping it hidden deep inside, hoping it never emerges, fearful of the destruction such a creature will have on those in its path. Hiding from our anger and fear is futile, and stuffing the emotions only serves to build the power of it when it does finally explode. Eventually someone or some event will come along and chink the wall enough that the anger will come pouring out.

Slaying this dragon of anger is futile as well. We cannot eliminate all things that make us angry or negate the pain and woundedness of our past. Instead we must stand in the center of the fire and not shrink back. We must confront our anger and fears courageously to see how we can grow from the experience. In the shamanic tradition, the initiate faces either a symbolic or real death experience as part of the transformation process. To come out as a stronger or wiser person you must retrieve the gift from the underworld, that is, to learn the lesson the experience has offered to teach you.

In order to find our true self we must search our "dark night of the soul." For many people this means hitting rock bottom before they can rebuild their lives or follow a healthier path. Many people are afraid to examine their lives because it often involves addressing their "shadow side," one's fears or life experiences that are unpleasant. In some cases, a spiritual director or therapist is needed to honestly examine one's self and learn new ways of achieving a healthy, balanced life. Only when we are willing to explore our best and worst characteristics can we freely choose which aspects of ourselves we want to bring into the world. From this process of intentional reflection and discernment, we can uncover our gifts and be more certain how to offer them to others.

I had a powerful experience of grieving that was instructive. I was dealing with a relationship loss that also tied into deeper feelings of childhood loss. I knew that I was keeping some strong emotions pretty tightly closed off, and that in order for me to move forward, I would need to release those feelings. I was having a sharp pain in my back and left shoulder so I went to a chiropractor hoping an alignment would help relieve it. In one session the doctor decided to do an acupuncture therapy with me as well. I'd had acupuncture sessions before so I thought it might help.

After the doctor put the needles in and left the room, I opened myself to whatever healing needed to be done. When the doctor came back I was still sitting in meditation. He pressed one needle in my left arm and it sent a shooting pain down my left arm and into my fingers. I screamed out and then my whole arm went numb momentarily. I started to cry. But at that moment I knew the pain wasn't a physical one. I knew I was tapping into a deeper emotional pain and that I was releasing the energy of it.

I asked the doctor to leave the room and let me sit alone. I reassured him I wasn't in physical pain but that I had some grieving to do. I cried for nearly an hour in his office. I knew there was more releasing I needed to do and was upset that I had to go to a meeting. I would need to stifle the grieving until later. I really wanted to be with the grief longer because I knew I was doing the releasing and cleansing work I needed to do. Over the next week, I had various occasions to grieve that were very healing for me. I was able to see the gift of releasing my grief so that I could move forward in a stronger way.

Instead of feeling we are battling with ourselves, we must accept that our fears and anger are a part of us. We must be present to our grief rather than run from it. We all have strengths *and* vulnerabilities. The light and the dark makes us whole. The path to greatness and spiritual growth involves facing our deeper, uncomfortable emotions, embracing them courageously, and learning to accept the gifts from them as a way to be stronger in the future.

Many people have had to confront their deepest fears; some return successfully from their inner underworld, others don't. Buckminster Fuller, one of the most renowned and influential thinkers of the twentieth century, had such a confrontation. Early in his adult life he was so disappointed with himself and felt so utterly discouraged, that he seriously considered suicide. On a walk along Lake Michigan at the age of 32, he wanted to throw himself into the dark waters because he felt his family would be better off without him. In the moment of facing his depth of despair, a voice within called out, "You do not have the right to eliminate yourself, you do not belong to you. You belong to the universe."[1]

Reflecting back on this event years later, he described how transformative that moment was:

> I vowed to keep myself alive, but only if I would never use me again for just me – I vowed to do my own thinking, instead of trying to accommodate everyone else's opinions, credos and theories. I vowed to apply my inventory of experiences to the solving of problems that affect everyone aboard planet Earth.... I'm absolutely convinced that everything that has happened to me since that time has been through my commitment to this greater integrity. Many times I've chickened out, and everything inevitably goes wrong. But then, when I return to my commitment, my life suddenly works again. There's something of the miraculous in that.[2]

Learning to face our own and others' anger and fears is one of our most basic life challenges. As luck or grace would have it, we continually get opportunities to perfect our response and learn the lessons. Work provides golden opportunities to confront our own or others' anger. Sometimes we walk away from such an experience the hero. At other times the dragon wins. We don't always effectively deal with our own or another's anger. Perhaps the fire is too hot or we feel too vulnerable.

Often we need more support in facing the dragon's fire. There is no rule that we have to face it alone. We need people to help us understand our own anger or deal with someone else's fears so we don't get burned. Trusted friends or support groups are extremely valuable in helping us confront the dragons in our lives. They also can help us determine when the fire is too hot and we need to retreat rather than be burned alive.

When the dragon wins, we must lick our wounds and learn from the situation. Sometime the wounds are quite deep and we have to turn our attention to the healing process before we can move forward.

GROUP AND ORGANIZATIONAL HEALING

In too many organizations today, due in part to broken trust, unexposed fears, or unleashed anger, people are hurting at a deep emotional and spiritual level. As a result, the organization can seem like a battlefield littered with casualties and few medics in sight. People and organizations won't reach their state of greatness when too much personal hurt and spiritual damage is done. Interpersonal and organizational healing often needs to happen to rebuild trust or provide strength to move forward successfully.

We must look within ourselves, individually and collectively, to determine what *we* can change to start the healing process. We need to let go of our harsh judgments of others or ourselves and muster the courage to try again. To accept and forgive our own and others' shortcomings, and heal from past wounds, we must retrieve the gifts from our own underworld. This is no small task. Again, we don't have to do it alone. We can draw to us trusted and wise friends or co-workers to help us in the process, to be guides or as support for our journey.

But if anyone has caused pain, he has caused it not to me, but in some measure to you all...so you should rather turn to forgive and comfort him, or he may be overwhelmed by excessive sorrow. So I beg you to affirm your love of him.

— 2 Corinthians 2:5-8

An important part of the healing process is understanding and awareness. When you get upset with someone who annoys you or causes you pain, try to figure out how *they* might be hurting. People intentionally hurt others because they feel hurt. They lash out in anger because they are angry inside. Lashing back only feeds fuel to the fire. A good affirmation when someone unfairly or harshly criticizes you is to say, "I wish for you joy not anger" or "Peace be with you." Take a personal vow to offer compassion and affirm another's Inner Light, rather than to criticize or judge in return. Be aware and summon the courage to go deep within yourself to see how the other person's anger triggers your own anger and pain. Find the strength and inspiration to bless and not to curse. An eye for an eye only leaves both people with less sight.

Another step is to set aside time to do healing work with the group(s) who are feeling the damage of broken trust or emotional pain from previous member or organizational actions. A half-day team building retreat can do wonders to getting people ready to *begin* to talk about the pain they feel. Once there is an opening for people to share their deeper feelings about what is going on in their work place, then healing can begin. Unless people feel safe to express their hurt from one another or from previous life experiences, the healing in the group won't happen.

Here are some questions for a group to answer as part of their healing process. A good way to facilitate this exercise is to use a focusing tool (e.g., a candle, stone, stick, or shell) to allow each person to share their thoughts and feelings without being interrupted or having others comment on what they say. People will need to feel they can share their views free of judgment from others. After all have shared their thoughts, the group can brainstorm ways to move forward.

1. When have we performed well? What conditions have helped us perform well?

2. What helps us keep motivated and inspired to do our best?

3. How are we vulnerable with each other? How do we feel about that vulnerability?

4. In what ways are we hurting from our experiences in this department or organization?

5. How have we hurt each other or let each other down?

6. How can we support each other's healing?

Groups that can answer these questions with one another take an enormous step towards their greater healing. Simply answering these questions openly and honestly indicates the group has some level of trust that can be built upon. When group members are ready to turn a corner and can answer these questions, they are on their way to rejuvenating their collective spirit.

Healing work takes time. Undoubtedly, the pain and actions that lead to feelings of hurt and mistrust don't happen all at once. Usually it builds slowly over the course of many months or years. Because the hurt and mistrust builds gradually, people may not notice it happening. Those who do notice may feel uncomfortable bringing it to the attention of the group and thus it never gets addressed. If this kind of mistrust and hurtful environment is deeply embedded in the organization's culture, then people won't even consider that the organization can function any other way. Too many people just accept that mistrust and hurtful relationships are status quo conditions in their organization. If the organizational culture rewards deceit and undercutting, then the healing won't take place without a major upheaval or extensive intervention.

Those groups that espouse principles of trust, respect, caring, etc. have at least some basis for rebuilding trust and starting their healing process. Most people feel uncomfortable saying or believing one thing and doing another. When it is brought up undeniably that people are not practicing what they preach, they often will look deeper at their actions and will want to start "walking the talk."

It takes a lot of effort to change patterns of behavior developed over a long period of time. However, if members are truly committed to doing their healing work, they must agree to support one another through the process. Just as in any healthy long-term relationship, members must have a true and deep commitment to want to heal. They need to set the intention and have the persistence to support one another through the healing process. They need to anticipate setbacks and be forgiving of each other when they falter along the way. It is important to provide encouragement for people to face their fears or past harm to continue moving forward. This healing work is essential if we are to serve others in love.

Reconciliation as Healing Work

Bill Moyers did a program for public television on the Truth and Reconciliation Committee in South Africa as that country tried to rebuild itself. I was impressed and overwhelmed at the idea that a government would institute such spiritual practices as a path to rebuild their country. They took as a basic premise that they would not move forward in a peaceful or healthy way unless they learned to forgive one another for past injury and that they must seek forgiveness for their part in perpetuating the pain. What a tremendous act of courage and spiritual enlightenment that process embodied. In the Moyers' program, it was so moving to see how people took steps to work through their deep hurting and emotional pain. In the reconciliation process, people who had murdered were brought before the families of those murdered to ask forgiveness. Both blacks and whites were brought before the committee. The tribunal that convened the process did not sit in judgment of guilt or innocence of the atrocities. Rather they were there to help the opposing parties seek reconciliation.

If it appeared that the offenders were truly genuine in their remorse and desire to be forgiven and could convince the family members of their atonement, then they were granted a pardon. Likewise the family members had to look deep within themselves to find the compassion and forgiveness necessary to move forward and accept the offenders' atonement. It took an enormous act of courage and compassion for both parties to come to terms with the violence that was committed.

Through reconciliation, the country was able to *begin* its healing work. This was a necessary step before people could begin to establish enough trust in a new system of governance and work to rebuild their country. Think how much stronger America would be if we went through this reconciliation to heal the pain of past oppression.

In less dramatic forms, reconciliation is needed in every day instances of trust being broken. In order to reestablish trust, there must be reconciliation.

Members of groups where there have been past wounds inflicted in the past must first open themselves to understanding the situation from one another's perspective. There must be empathy to see why someone acted as they did. Their actions may very well have been immoral or unprincipled. However, if we go deeper we may begin to see why they felt a need to act in unscrupulous ways. Usually upon deeper examination, they acted out of self protection because they felt fear of being hurt. The Dalai Lama teaches that unless we understand the suffering of others we will not be able to offer compassion to them.

I am a circle, I am healing you.

You are a circle, you are healing me.

United we are One.

United we are as One.

— Native American Indian chant

We must be open to understanding and empathy to see the suffering of others in order to offer our forgiveness. For group healing to take place, each person who has caused pain to another must look deep within to understand her own actions. They must acknowledge their role in creating the wounds and offer atonement for their part of the pain. Through atonement for our own actions, empathy, and understanding of others, we come to a place of greater compassion and forgiveness for wrongdoing. We must acknowledge our own and others' emotional scars to begin our healing process and rebuild the relationships.

Reconciliation must be done with a healing intention from all parties involved. Reconciliation with the spiritual intent to heal is different from traditional conflict resolution techniques. Below is an example of how to do this in a group.

When doing reconciliation in a work group, each party involved should first admit small transgressions to one another. After the disputing parties share their smaller transgression, in silence they turn inward to find compassion and acknowledge the damage done. They seek healing for themselves and for the other. It may be that the other party is not ready to offer forgiveness yet, or that each party does not acknowledge the entirety of the damage done. Each party should offer whatever form of forgiveness, understanding, or empathy they can to the other. Each party must ask for healing to occur and affirm the healing process even if they don't feel ready to admit full blame or grant full forgiveness. If they feel able to speak of other transgressions they should do so. In this way more significant hurtful actions can be addressed. Healing will only come from seeking atonement and releasing anger and resentment.

Once the healing starts, people can seek more and different ways to offer compassionate understanding and form more trusting relationships. Look for opportunities in your work place to be forgiving or offer your compassionate understanding to others. As mentioned previously, honesty, integrity, forgiveness, and courage are essential ingredients to re-build relationships. These characteristics must be supported, nurtured, modeled, and rewarded at work. Individuals must be open to this healing work for healing to take place. It cannot be forced.

FINDING THE GIFTS IN OTHERS'
SHORTCOMINGS

Several years ago, I heard this story about a group who learned to see what gifts each had to offer. I love to share this story because it illustrates that while people in our work group have weaknesses and irritating qualities, we must also look for their gifts as well.

There was a monastery that had been a thriving place to study and live for nearly two hundred years. For the past twenty years the monastery was slowly dying by its inability to attract new initiates and the death of older monks. This left just four monks to tend to the grounds and maintain the teachings and practice of the monastery. These remaining four monks were also old and tired and worried about how the monastery would survive. Due to these stresses they often were bitter and critical of one another.

One day Brother Stephen was walking in the oak grove past the garden when he came upon a stranger. He was surprised by the stranger because he hadn't seen a car at the office when he left. He approached the stranger and welcomed him to the monastery.

"Is this your first visit to our monastery?" Brother Stephen asked.

"No, I've been here many times before," the stranger replied. "It is always so beautiful here. I come here to feel the peacefulness of the place."

The stranger continued, "But you know, it hasn't seemed so peaceful lately. I've felt some tension, some difficulties here."

Brother Stephen was a little embarrassed by this comment. "Well we are getting older and it's been a strain on us."

"I am surprised by the troubles you are having with each other. You know *the messiah is amongst you.*"

Brother Stephen was so surprised he looked away as he spoke, "The messiah is amongst us, what do you mean by that?" And as he turned back to face the stranger no one was there.

Brother Stephen couldn't believe his eyes and wondered if he hadn't been out in the garden too long that morning. He thought the stress of the monastery had perhaps taken more of a toll on his health than he imagined. He walked slowly back to the monastery in deep reflection.

That night during dinner and evening prayers the other monks noticed Brother Stephen lost in thought. For the next few days Brother Stephen seemed preoccupied and not his normal self. A week later during community meeting, Brother Michael asked him what was on his mind.

Brother Stephen explained the episode and shared that he wasn't sure if it had really happened or not. He didn't quite know what to make of the message that "the messiah is amongst us." The other monks were also unsure and reflected on the story.

Over the next few weeks each monk contemplated the meaning of the episode. Brother Michael sometimes resented Brother Stephen because he felt Brother Stephen was too pious at times. 'Perhaps I have been too critical of him,' Brother Michael thought. 'I need to try to understand him better.'

Likewise, Brother James thought that Brother Michael was sometimes too critical and wasn't as forgiving as he could be. 'But am I also being too harsh?', he thought. 'Perhaps Brother Michael has something to teach me that is the way of the messiah. I need to be more forgiving of Michael's imperfections.'

As Brother James was more forgiving, Brother Thomas saw he had been too judgmental of Brother James. Brother Thomas often found himself annoyed because he didn't feel Brother James was contemplative enough. He felt that Brother

James seemed too joyful at times to be taken seriously as a monk. But he looked within himself and realized he needed to find joy in his work to continue to support the monastery.

And so it was that the four monks, each striving to find what they could within each other that represented the messiah, found aspects of themselves they needed to change. Over time the monks treated each other with more reverence, joy, forgiveness, and compassion. They looked for the divinity in each other.

The energy and atmosphere of the monastery shifted. Visitors could feel the joyfulness and compassion of the monks. Guests who had been to the monastery in recent years could feel the change. More people were attracted to the monastery to experience the peacefulness and the presence of the monks. Slowly the monks healed their past injuries and the monastery healed in turn. New students came to learn about the life and teachings of the monks. New initiates joined. The monastery returned to being a thriving spiritual community.

The story of the monastery is an example of an organization that was slowly dying but then able to heal and turn itself around by finding the gifts in one another's apparent weaknesses.

Through commitment, honesty, forgiveness, and support, group members can rebuild trust, improve relationships, and heal from past damages. Organizations that see their role in helping people find greater wholeness and grow spiritually ultimately will flourish. To follow the path to greatness you must take responsibility for your healing and make personal changes to deal with past injuries.

The healing and reconciliation process involves honest self-examination of actions we have taken that have damaged our relationships. Sometimes we won't forgive someone else because we insist we were right and they were wrong. We don't want to acknowledge our own missteps. The best way to offer forgiveness is to see what you have done to cause injury to another. This is an important step in your path for greatness.

First, we must look honestly at what we have done to feed the problems or hurt feelings. Then we must take ownership of the pain we have caused. We must ask forgiveness of ourselves as well. Look at it as an opportunity to learn and grow, not as a damnation of yourself. The minute you beat yourself up for your misdeeds, you focus on the negative rather than the positive growth. Learning won't happen then. Healing comes in seeing the wounds clearly and in offering forgiveness to yourself and others, while taking responsibility for doing better next time and accepting the consequences of your actions.

To know true freedom...we all, sooner or later, must make the choice to forgive.

– Robin Casarjian

EXERCISES

1. Reconciliation as a group can be a powerful process for greater healing. This exercise should be done with a trained facilitator who can guide the group through the pain or conflicts presented. The facilitator must remind the group they are doing this to heal and not to blame, to affirm growth rather than punish.

   The primary parties who were involved in a dispute or hurtful situation should sit in the center of a circle. Other people affected by these transgressions sit around the primary parties. The outer group is there to offer support for the disputing parties to seek reconciliation. They are to sit without comment or judgment. The circle of supporters form an accepting community to this healing process. Having the outer circle as witness to the reconciliation, the primary parties not only see how their actions affect a larger circle but know they will need to be accountable to others.

   After the first round of admitting transgressions and seeking forgiveness, others may come to sit in the center of the circle to take responsibility and acknowledge the role they had in supporting the damaging relationships. This may lead to new transgressions being acknowledged and wider healing taking place.

2. Consider signing and/or posting this type of pledge at your workplace. Feel free to change the words so that you have a pledge that will guide your day.

I pledge to work spiritually intentionally by doing the following. I will:

Refrain from using hostile words when
I am hurt

Search for greater understanding when
others attack or criticize me

Seek compassion and forgiveness of myself
or others when I or they fall short

Stay connected to my Source of inspiration
when I am upset or angry

Remember that I can act as a beacon of
Divine Love

15

ORGANIZATIONAL RITUALS AND RITES OF PASSAGE

*Our ideal for a society, in other words, is not that it should be a
perfectly static organization, founded in the age of the
ancestors and to remain unchanging through all time. It is
rather of a process moving toward a fulfillment of as yet
unrealized possibilities; and in this living process each is to be an
initiating yet cooperative center.*

– Joseph Campbell, *Myths to Live By*

My definition of spirituality includes having a sense of
wholeness, meaning, and connection. Most
organizations have fairly sterile rituals that do little to inspire
people, let alone leave them with a sense of wholeness,
meaning, and connection to one another. As people look for
work that is spiritually fulfilling, organizations must recognize
their role as being an arena for that spiritual growth to occur.
Rituals are powerful ways to help people find connections to

others and to connect to organizational values and principles. By creating and participating in more meaningful rituals, we find ways to offer our gifts and passion in service to others.

This chapter examines how rituals are used to bring about a greater sense of belonging and connection to the organization. In addition, I suggest ways in which rites of passage, as a specific type of ritual, can be used effectively to deal with changes within an organization and create a greater sense of belonging and meaning.

CULTURE AND RITUALS

A culture is generally understood to include a set of shared beliefs and assumptions, implicit rules to organize society, and the common characteristics of a population. A custom is a long established practice considered as unwritten law or convention that regulates social life, whereas a ritual is an established form of ceremony or any formal, repeated act. Cultures are exemplified by their rituals, not only in what the rituals are but what the rituals represent to the people involved. Because organizations are social institutions, rituals play a significant role in expressing meaning in the organization.

An organization's culture is revealed by its symbols and stories, rituals and customs. Through stories and legends, the organizational history is told and members learn what is important in the organization. Storytelling occurs at annual meetings, in newsletters, and in annual reports. These stories make the values of the organization real and known to organizational members.

Customs and rituals are one way in which companies "walk their talk." The symbolic ways people interact with one another in meetings and gatherings speak volumes for what is truly valued in organizations. For example, the way people sit around a table reflects how important status and hierarchy is to the organization.

Rituals are powerful tools for expressing the values and principles within an organization. For example, the way employee recognition is given (or not given) should be examined in every organization. If the organization gives plaques and awards to star players but the company wants to value team effort, then the message sent is that stars are more important to the organization than working as a team. Another common value espoused by organizations is employee input for continuous improvement. Therefore the company can include a ceremony showing the ways in which employee input was helpful to the organization. This builds meaning into one's work as service to a larger good.

Rituals reveal both what employees think and feel about the organization as well as what messages the organization conveys to its employees. An example of a ritual many organizations have is a door decorating contest at Christmas time. This activity often is meant to embrace the holiday spirit and provide a creative outlet for people in the worksite. Much can be learned from this ritual, not only by which people participate, but what is acknowledged in this ritual.

One organization going through serious morale problems and high turnover engaged in door decorating, and it proved to be very enlightening. Judges for the door decorating contest walked down the hall and were struck by the images portrayed. Many doors had themes such as Scrooge, the Grinch, and the Misfit Toyland. The cynicism and even pain employees were feeling at the time were obvious. This ritual provided an outlet for those feelings to be expressed. Luckily for this organization, the judges were top managers in a position to address employee concerns and direct resources to deal with the morale problems.

Current organizational rituals need to be carefully examined to understand what values are represented and what messages are conveyed. Many organizations are spending enormous amounts of time and energy writing vision and mission statements. While these exercises are fruitful in that they help organizations clarify what they are there to do, unless the mission and vision is embodied in the culture and through rituals, the statements are merely words on paper. Rituals need to be done intentionally to convey the values and important ideas of an organization. There needs to be some formal ceremony or activity to reinforce the mission if the organization truly wants to live it.

As long as there are tests, there will always be prayer in school.

– Bumper Sticker

Earlier I discussed trust as key to healthy work group relations and organizational effectiveness. Several rituals can be done to help groups function better. The fishbowl exercise could be done periodically as an organizational ritual and not just used to address a crisis. A denominational group I helped form, C-UUYAN (Continental Unitarian Universalist Young Adult Network), meets annually at a week-long summer conference. During several years that I attended the conference, people looked forward to doing a fishbowl exercise each year. It became a ritual that was a powerful event to bind the community. Other trust-building activities can be done in a ceremonial way so that members recognize that trust is valued in the organization. Retreats are good times to perform such rituals.

The way meetings start often sets the tone for the rest of the meeting. People who rush from one meeting to another often don't have time to focus on the task at hand, barely clearing their head from their previous meetings. A short ritual of silence or ringing a chime or bell can help people regain some focus. Silence is an effective tool for gathering one's thoughts and focusing on the present.

I worked with one group where the members met monthly and came from various parts of the city for the meetings. They were all busy people running their own organizations. After the first few meetings it was apparent that the group took about 20 minutes to get focused. Since we usually had a long agenda and wanted to finish in an hour and a half, I knew I needed to do something as facilitator to get them to focus quicker. To one meeting I brought brown lunch bags and asked everyone to take one. I asked them to write on a piece of paper all the things they were thinking of when they walked in the room. They were told to write on the paper all those events and activities that were weighing on their minds and then put the paper in the bag. After they did this, I told them to fold the bag and put it underneath their seats.

I told them they could get the bag and all their other thoughts at the end of the meeting but for now they needed to focus on what our meeting was about. The meeting went very smoothly that morning because people were much more focused. Several people commented at the end that they thought the brown bag helped them put aside their worries and concerns about other matters.

Another ritual for focusing and channeling the group energy is to pass a candle or talking stick around the room and allow people to share 2 to 3 sentences about how they are feeling that day or what may be distracting them. Having a moment of silence between each speaker provides an opportunity for their words and energy to be directed or released as necessary. This type of beginning provides a chance for people to focus the energy of the group.

You can do a personal ritual at the beginning of a meeting while people gather. Close your eyes, pay attention to your breathing, and say a silent prayer for harmonious relations between all those present, for insightful thinking and clarity, and for connection with the Divine Source. A group can create an affirmation or centering words that they say silently or out loud to help them focus on their meeting time together.

Before a group meeting you could ask others to join you in doing a visualization such as bringing Light into the room and collecting everyone's energy to a focal point in the room. See the Light guide the group to its Higher Truth. By doing this, the energy of the group is raised to new levels.

Rituals, like pep rallies, can raise energy levels of the group and focus a team on its task. Time should be spent to allow individuals to focus on the group and tasks ahead as well as to connect with their Source. This time for focus and centering allows people to constructively channel their energy so that their personal agendas and personal distractions can be minimized.

The common characteristics of ritual are:

1. Rituals are intentionally done (not activities done out of habit)

2. Rituals raise awareness of experiences and feelings

3. Rituals involve physical, mental (cognitive), emotional, and spiritual elements

Most people think of rituals as connection to the Divine. In many places of worship, there are elaborate rituals for the individual to connect to the Divine directly or connect to the organization that performs Divine work or teaches about the Divine. Rituals can also be done to connect the individual to a community and break down feelings of isolation and alienation. Initiation rituals are part of the process to belonging to a group and feeling accepted.

Rituals emphasize what is valued in the culture and expresses the commonality of the membership. Rituals validate individual feelings and honor the individual. They show change as necessary and part of the life experience. Rituals also mark profound events. Rites of passage, as a type of ritual, can be used in organizations to designate key activities in the life of an organization or its members.

RITES OF PASSAGE

Getting a driver's license, graduating from high school, and starting your first job are all events that mark passages into adulthood. It is perhaps unintended in America that the final designation of entering adulthood is the ability to drink alcohol legally. Various social workers want more meaningful rituals created for youth to welcome them into their communities and into adulthood in positive and meaningful ways. Organizations serving youth would do well to develop such rites of passage or borrow ideas from various cultures throughout history for rituals that have welcomed youth into the adult community.

A rite of passage is a ritual associated with a crisis or a change of status for an individual. Given this definition, it is easy to see how rites of passage would apply to organizations. Anyone who has tried to implement widespread organizational change knows that employee resistance is the biggest hurdle. Rites of passage can be used effectively to help employees not only find meaning in these changes but feel prepared for them.

As organizations continually change to meet customer demands and competitive forces, they face internal crisis and change of status repeatedly. Rites are extremely important to help people work through their emotions during a time of change or crisis. It is likely that if the rites are not provided, the change will not take place in a healthy, productive way.

Rites of passage can be profoundly important to help individuals deal with change, provided they are consistent with the values of the people involved and performed with the intention of helping the individuals involved move through the changes in a meaningful way. In his book *Myths to Live By*, Joseph Campbell described how JFK's funeral was a significant rite of passage to help Americans with their loss and to work through the grieving process. More recently, the people of England urged their monarchy to support them in their grieving process by providing a proper funeral and ceremony for the passing of Lady Diana.

Likewise, in all areas of human social intercourse, ritualized procedures depersonalize the protagonists, drop or lift them out of themselves, so that their conduct now is not their own but of the species, the society, the caste, or the profession.

– Joseph Campbell

While the above are fairly dramatic examples of grieving and rites of passage, more common examples of crisis and change frequently occur in organizations. The emotional impact of such events should not be minimized. Symbolic deaths and grieving happen when people retire, lose their jobs, or have their jobs restructured. Those employees who remain after downsizing often experience guilt and negative emotions that need to be addressed. The emotional toll on employees during times of downsizing or restructuring must be dealt with for the change process to take place smoothly. Likewise, during good times organizations need to help employees celebrate their achievements to feel a sense of accomplishment and recognition for their work.

ORGANIZATIONAL RITES OF PASSAGE

Four common organizational events that would be better served with rites of passage are: new employee entrance, promotion or job restructuring, formation of self-directed teams, and exiting (voluntarily or not). Rites of passage can be developed for these activities to recognize them as a time of change, to provide personal meaning for the change, to connect members to one another, and to raise awareness of the opportunity for personal growth. Certainly there are other events that merit rituals (e.g., corporate mergers). I suggest you examine your organization and determine if a significant event would be made more meaningful and go more smoothly if you had a rite of passage.

Far too many employees start their job with little or no initiation. Many employees are thrown into work with little training but perhaps a walk around the work area and an introduction to some key co-workers. Some organizations provide a lunch or breakfast as an opportunity to meet the new hire and provide a social event for the company. Little, if anything, is said to the new employee about the values of the company. There is no discussion of the dreams and expectations of the employee and his role in creating them in the company.

The new employee often walks in cold to this new community of people and is expected to learn on the job while figuring out, and hopefully accepting, the culture and values of the organization. Human Resource managers know that new employees go through a socialization process, but little is offered in the form of creating rites of passage to make that process intentional and effective.

A rite of passage could take place in the final interview and job acceptance stage. A common "ritual" at this stage involves negotiating salary and benefits, with some discussion of what the job expectations will be regarding tasks and duties. However, many expectations of the employee and the organization are left unspoken with respect to what values, norms, or principles are shared. Rarely is the employee asked to accept the vision and mission of the organization in a ceremonial way. Even less often is the organization involved in a ritual to show how it will live out its vision, mission, and principles with the employee. Think how much more powerfully the vision, mission, and principles would be embraced if a simple ceremony existed in the organization for this occasion.

An example of this type of ceremony is seen in many churches when they undergo a covenanting process when they call a new minister. During this process, the church members state what they expect from a new minister and what they intend to do to support that minister. Likewise, the minister declares what she will do to support the life of the church. Such a covenanting process solidifies the relationship and demonstrates that everyone is working for the common good of the church and that all members are responsible for the life of the church. Since many churches only keep a minister five to ten years, it doesn't matter that the relationship may be short lived. What matters is that the relationship is grounded in a sense of commitment, community, and meaning.

Even during times of uncertainty and restructuring, or perhaps especially because of such uncertainty, businesses likewise would do well to undergo such a covenanting process with their employees. Many employees want more than pay for their work; they want to feel accepted and honored for who they are and what they do. As businesses expect more and better quality work from their employees with little extra money or security to offer in exchange, a meaningful process such as rituals can be put in place to keep employees motivated and committed.

The essence of Total Quality Management (TQM) is to make continuous improvement in the organization's culture, process, and technology in an environment of trust and openness. TQM focuses on customers, both internal and external, to the organization. TQM steps to increase internal customer satisfaction can be augmented by various rituals. Developing rituals around what the organization promises its employees and what employees promise their organization will move members into new levels of cooperation and commitment. A new hire orientation that includes ritual can be effective in building commitment to the organization at the outset and can provide an opportunity to build bonds between the new employee and his colleagues.

Promotions and job restructuring likewise are times of status change for the individuals involved. Rites of passage can be implemented to convey the new employee's role in the organization or department. Most employees have some sense of what new job assignments they will have and what their duties are, but few are prepared for the emotional and relationship changes that will take place. Rites of passage can specifically address these so that not only the person being promoted has a better understanding of these changes, but those who are affected by the changes can acknowledge the transition.

It is not uncommon for operation crews to become tight-knit groups, clans if you will. Crews can become so tight-knit in fact that there is pressure not to change the composition of group members for fear that the intimacy and stability will be lost. In one organization where the crews had been working together for years, the department head offered training so his workers could get promotions to higher paying jobs. Despite the best intentions and efforts of the department head, the crew members didn't participate.

Without understanding the social interactions and group pressures involved, the department head was left frustrated and disappointed that his training series was so poorly attended. His interpretation was that people did not want more responsibility or expanded job duties. Once he understood that people did not want to leave their clans and change the status of group members, he was able to restructure his training program and publicize it better to allay the fears associated with the changed status. A rite of passage for all the members of the group would help the initiate who is being promoted accept his or her changed status. It would also help the other members let go of the initiate, and accept the changed status, if not celebrate it.

Rites of passage can be useful tools for acknowledging the emotions, honoring the change process, and focusing on the change as an opportunity for growth among all members.

Similarly, self-directed teams will only be as successful as the team members' ability to accept each other's change of status. A necessary component to self-directed teams is to have the former supervisor accept her changed role. However, most companies rarely address the emotional impact of such changes for the supervisor and group members. Rites of passage can be useful tools for acknowledging the emotions, honoring the change process, and focusing on the change as an opportunity for growth among all members.

Team building exercises that include rituals are effective because they reveal emotions people have about their changed status and roles. Without understanding and recognizing these changes at a deeper level, problems will continually emerge and people will be left frustrated and confused as to how to correct them. Allowing employees to create rites of passage for their group to acknowledge the changes involved will help them channel their fears or excitement into a constructive process for all. The ritual should entail an activity for members to search for ways they can grow spiritually with one another.

Finally, rites of passage can be useful during the exiting stage of the employee life cycle with an organization. Whether the exit is through retirement, layoff, or job relocation, both the employee and those left behind benefit from a rite of passage ceremony. Even if everyone feels positive about the exit, or sees it as a good launch for the employee to her next stage of development, more needs to be done to uncover the range of feelings that may be associated with it and constructively direct those feelings. Rites of passage ceremonies can acknowledge the loss, honor the individual, or reinforce group values and norms. This provides a stage for unspoken feelings or expectations to surface that otherwise may not surface, or worse still, arise in unexpected or destructive ways.

As downsizing occurs, managers need to be aware not only of the effects of the lost job on the people who are let go, but they also must address the emotional toll it takes on those who stay.[1] Organizational survivors must be supported because they either feel guilt over still having their jobs or anger at losing their colleagues. Preparing a ritual for those who survive a downsizing effort would be beneficial to reduce the emotional toll and anxiety felt during that difficult time. Likewise, those people who are downsized will need to put closure on their relationship with the co-workers and process the experience of separation from the company. A ritual is very valuable to allow that closure to happen. Without it, organizations run the risk of retaliation, including violence, from laid-off workers.

In addition, since many high performers start looking for other work during a downsizing, a ritual designed to affirm their importance to the organization might help in reducing the exodus of good workers. Rather than send the message of "you're lucky to still have a job," a ritual could be designed to work through any pain or damage done from the downsizing, as well as help those who survive adjust to the change and prepare for a new work environment. Healing will be needed in these circumstances; rituals help facilitate that healing process.

Many organizations provide "going away" or retirement parties for employees who leave on their own behalf. Such a party could incorporate a time for people not only to express what they feel about the employee leaving, but provide an opportunity for the employee to reflect on what this transition will mean in her life. Again, acknowledging the change of status and the community's role in supporting that change is critical for the change to go smoothly. Gifts or tokens of appreciation are often exchanged, but organizations can be more intentional about what the gifts represent not only for the individual, but also what organizational values are represented. These types of ceremonies do not need to be lavish, lengthy, or expensive to convey to the remaining employees that people are important to the organization and to reaffirm the values and principles of the organization.

Most of the rites of passage that can be created must be built on a common set of values and norms of the group. As organizations become more diverse, values will differ across groups. Groups who share a history of experiences will develop their own values and norms. In order for the rite of passage to be meaningful, the ritual must be tailored to the unique characteristics of the group. At the same time, rites of passage can reflect universal values of respect, caring, trust, and belonging. The different rites of passage that organizations create are purely open to the creativity of those group members involved. Certain key elements should be included and intentionally reflected upon when the rite is constructed. These key elements are:

1. Symbols used to represent the desired values held by the group or organization.

2. Opening and closing activities to show the bonds that unite the people involved and creating safe space for people to be open with their emotions.

3. Activities to honor the change of status of the initiate as well as the change for the group members affected.

4. Time to share or reflect on the emotions people have about the change.

SUMMARY

Both the organizational culture and its rituals impact organizational members in how they find meaning in their work and in how they connect to one another. Leaders and team members must be mindful of the influence the organizational culture has on individual performance and group relations through stories, ceremonies, and symbols used. Be aware of the messages conveyed to employees about what is important and valued in your organization, and then create rituals that support these values. It is especially important to recognize the rituals and messages that undermine or conflict with the values espoused by the organization.

Rituals that are carefully planned and intentional help build a sense of belonging to a larger group. Rites of passage can help connect people to one another and the larger organization. In addition, rites also help organizations progress through change more smoothly. Rites of passage provide an opportunity to express feelings and find meaning in the necessary transitions in organizational life. Through the transitions and significant events in our work life, we learn new ways of being and are provided opportunities for growth. Organizations that want to foster the growth of their members will be creative in developing meaningful rituals. Rituals become important times for people to grow spiritually together.

EXERCISES

1. Plan a ritual for your work group. Consider the following as you decide what to do.

   a. What organizational or group values do you want to emphasize?

   b. What are commonly shared characteristics and/or differences within your group?

   c. What symbols would represent the values or characteristics of your group?

   d. What types of activity (physical, emotional, mental) do you want to include?

   e. How can you bring in symbols or activities that all can use to connect with the Divine?

   f. What kind of feelings or messages do you want participants to retain when they leave?

2. Conduct a ritual with your group or organization.

   a. Who should be involved in planning the ritual?

   b. How will you open and close the ceremony/activity?

   c. Where will you conduct it, what setting best serves the ceremony?

   d. Who should participate in the ceremony?

   e. Are there leaders or distinct roles for people? If so, how will you prepare them for their tasks?

3. Select a key event or transition in your group or organization that needs greater acknowledgment and plan a rite of passage around it (using same guidelines as above).

References for further reading on rituals:

Beck, Renee, and Sydney Barbara Metrick *The Art of Ritual,* Berkeley CA, New World Library, 1990.

Brooks, Nan *Ceremonies for Our Lives*, Spirit Magic Books, Bloomington IN, 1991.

Imber-Black, Evan, and Janine Roberts *Rituals for Our Times: Celebrating, Healing, and Changing Our Lives and Our Relationships,* NY, HarperCollins, 1992.

Klein, Tzipora *Celebrating Life: Rites of Passage for All Ages*, Delphi Press, Oak Park, IL 1992.

PART IV

ORGANIZATIONS AS ARENAS FOR SPIRITUAL GROWTH

16

NEW VS. OLD PARADIGMS

In new organizations structure will not be a state but a process.

— Rolf Osterberg. *Corporate Renaissance*

As more people aspire to develop themselves spiritually, they want to have co-workers and supervisors who see the value of spiritual growth. An increasing number of people who see career counselors want to leave dead-end jobs or toxic work environments to find jobs and companies that feed them spiritually. When people take seriously their call to become more authentic spiritual beings, they seek work environments and organizations that support their spiritual journey.

People who want to grow spiritually through their work are seeking what I call Higher Consciousness Organizations (HCOs). Paychecks and job security are not enough for people who want to bring their gifts and passion to their work. Business Week highlighted several companies, such as AT&T, Lotus, and Boeing, that are taking steps to build spirituality at work as a means to help motivate their employees, increase creativity, or develop new leadership skills.[1] A growing New York company, Agency.com, started a program called "InspireU," an in-house "university" designed by employees who wanted to offer their gifts in more ways than their usual daily interactions allowed.[2]

Organizations interested in attracting employees who are creative, willing to take risks, work with more energy, and be able to change as new demands arise, need to develop cultures and structures to support such workers. This is particularly true for the new entrants into the workforce, Generation Xers. Since the Gen Xers don't expect lifetime employment, they want to use their talents and grow or else they won't stay with a company. As a result, companies need to offer workshops and experiences for their employees to help them grow as spiritual human beings. [3]

In a discussion with an executive of a longstanding Fortune 500 company, she lamented to me that many good middle managers were leaving for lucrative job offers with dot-com companies. I told her that her company may not be able to compete on salary but could keep good people by having a work environment that helped people feel fulfilled through their work. Quality work and committed workers are a result of companies supporting the wholeness of their people. This is a significant shift from traditional work environments during the twentieth century.

Changing views of Employees

throughout the Twentieth Century

For centuries, artisans and farmers saw themselves through their trade and creations. Their identity was directly linked to their craft. They saw the full creation of their work from seed to grain, from piece of wood to carriage wheel. In seeing the production process from raw material to completed product, they were able to experience wholeness and connection to work. In the nineteenth and twentieth centuries, the industrial revolution was a boon to economic development. However, new forms of technology took away many people's sense of wholeness and connection of self in work.

At the beginning of the twentieth century, factory owners turned to efficiency experts to help improve productivity. In 1911 Frederick Taylor published his book *Principles of Scientific Management*, which codified a new approach to managing workers in the industrial age. The Scientific Management approach reduced workers to a quantifiable unit in an organization.

During this same time, Max Weber established the bureaucracy as the ideal type of efficient organization. Though Weber feared that bureaucratic settings would result in organizations becoming "an iron cage" that would strip away individualism, bureaucracies became the model against which all organizations were measured for maximum efficiency. Thus, the combination of Taylor and Weber's work resulted in the paradigm of organizations as scientific bureaucracies that limited job tasks, regimented activities and relationships, and created hierarchies of control which reduced individual involvement and responsibility at work. From this model, the "new organizations" of the twentieth century were born.[4]

Scholars in the Human Resources and Organizational Behavior fields in subsequent decades focused on the social, psychological, and technical implications of work in the industrial era. Realizing the limitations of the scientific bureaucracies, Douglas McGregor's influential work in the 1950s called for a Theory Y management alternative to the Scientific Management approach. Along with Abraham Maslow, McGregor helped found the Human Relations movement. The basic premises underlying the Human Relations movement were that motivation depends on social needs more so than economic needs, and the social environment had a significant impact on workers. McGregor's Theory Y prescribed giving people greater responsibility and autonomy under the assumption that people would naturally find work as important as rest or play. As a result of McGregor's and Maslow's scholarship, a ground swell of research and consulting has been done to make work places more meaningful and productive.

Juxtaposed to the Human Relations movement in the 1950s was the commonly held but mistaken notion that an employee's job performance was not affected by his personal life. The "organizational man" was an employee who was supposed to punch the clock and leave any thoughts of family or personal issues at home. Later research on the topic of "Work Life – Family Life Satisfaction" found that balancing work and home life demands was a major concern to workers, and the lack of balance impacted their productivity.

The field of Organization Development (OD) blossomed in the 1970s as an extension of the Human Relations movement. OD practitioners applied various interventions to promote team building and trust building in organizations. Job enrichment programs, and more recently self-directed teams, are interventions that build on the field of OD and the Human Relations movement. Similarly, the trend of job restructuring, begun in the 1970s to bring back "task identity" and "task significance" was an important first step in reestablishing the sense of wholeness in one's work. Also in the 1970s, William Ouchi's Theory Z borrowed from Japanese management, calling for management to treat workers as family and emphasizing work as a contribution to the whole.

Despite the results of decades of research, many organizations have failed to recognize that their members are their greatest assets to be nurtured and developed. Too often, long-term employee development gives way to the pressures from short-term quarterly gains. For years, the "holy canon" of business, espoused by such influential people as Milton Friedman, was that businesses exist only to make money for the Shareholders. As long as this view still prevails in most executives' *and* employees' minds, the pressure for short term financial gains will almost always take priority over long term personal and interpersonal growth.

The civil rights and environmental movements of the 1960s and 1970s highlighted the notion that businesses serve tandem purposes: the shareholders and society. Thus the "Holy Canon" of business was challenged publicly. In the 1980s, business schools began teaching the concept of "Corporate Social Responsibility" and offering business ethics courses. "Corporate Social Responsibility" is based on the view that corporations must balance the needs of society with serving shareholder interests. This view brought forth the concept of Stakeholders in addition to Stockholders. Employees and citizens are two important Stakeholders in the corporate responsibility framework.

Business for Social Responsibility (BSR) is an association of businesses that accept the basic concepts and principles of corporate social responsibility. BSR espouses a stakeholder approach, whereby the organization strives to satisfy customers, employees, and society, in addition to shareholders. A founding member of BSR, Tom Chappell believes that spirit has to inform business and that there has to be a broader perspective than the bottom line. This broader set of goals includes the environment, employees, customers, and the bottom line. According to Chappell, there is an added burden of expectations in using the stakeholder approach. But he believes that you have to defer to a power greater than yourself that will guide you to be involved in the process.

For six years you shall sow your land and gather its yield; but the seventh year you shall let it rest and lie fallow, that the poor of our people may eat.

— Exodus 23:10-11

During the 1980s and 1990s, OD practitioners began to use spiritual ideas to help organizations change. In the book *World Waiting to Be Born*, M. Scott Peck describes his efforts to bring civility into the workplace and the success organizations have when they do so. Peck is clear in his definition that civility involves connecting to a Higher Power. Through his work with organizations he describes a process that makes space for the Grace of God to enter work relationships so that people can be honest and trusting with their co-workers.

Rolf Osterberg, a successful Swedish media executive, champions a new role for businesses and corporations in the twenty-first century. In *Corporate Renaissance*, Osterberg urges readers to more carefully scrutinize the free market economic system. He challenges the profit motive as the primary reason for business' existence. Rather than profits being the bottom line, he advocates for businesses and organizations to become arenas for growth first and foremost.

Similarly, Aaron Feuerstein refers to the book of Exodus to suggest that there are limits on wealth. In Exodus 23:10-11, "For six years you shall sow your land and gather its yield; but the seventh year you shall let it rest and lie fallow, that the poor of our people may eat."

There is a maximum point at which profits exceed the larger social expense. For example, should society allow corporations to make a profit by externalizing the costs of damage to the environment? Rather than internalizing the cost of cleaning up the environment or correcting a social problem they create, corporations frequently pass off the problem to local communities or states. Often organizational actions are so far removed from our actions as consumers and citizens that we don't feel responsible for the problem. We don't get very alarmed unless a problem affects us personally. But can we as consumers shed our responsibility when we purchase products that are harmful for the environment or come from poor working conditions?

From a spiritual orientation the answer is clearly no. When we begin to see ourselves as One (One with each other and with God) we see more clearly how organizations impact us, either by their impact on the planet and the earth's resources, or through workplace relations and meaningful work. We cannot separate ourselves from what organizations do. By being more fully spiritual beings we can help organizations serve their Highest Good.

Clearly, there was great change over the course of the twentieth century regarding how organizations viewed themselves and their members. Issues of worker health and safety, productivity, and job satisfaction are still important. But as we enter the twenty-first century, a new Human Relations movement is underway, a movement that recognizes that people are motivated by spiritual principles.

Stephen Covey, Tom Chappell, and others assert that organizations guided by values and principles that are accepted by its members will be best able to survive in turbulent times. I propose that spiritual principles, such as compassion, forgiveness, mindfulness, and atonement are important for personal and organizational transformation. In order for organizations to thrive, particularly in crisis situations, many people rely on faith to take actions that run counter to the status quo or "conventional wisdom." Deeper Wisdom is often required in these cases. This wisdom can be found in various texts and teachings that have guided behavior for thousands of years.

WORKING SPIRITUALLY IN TRADITIONAL

ORGANIZATIONS

How can people work more spiritually in traditional organizations? Find ways in which your work is service to others and to God. If you are committed to your spiritual growth, you can practice your spirituality in most work environments. By applying the ideas and practicing the activities outlined earlier in this book, you will find ways to work spiritually, even in difficult situations. Using the ideas outlined in this book, you will move further along in your spiritual journey no matter what job you have.

Search for those individuals in your organization who similarly want to grow spiritually. I shared a draft version of my book with a secretary who worked in a department with morale problems. As a result of doing some of the exercises in my book, she was able to improve her attitude about her work. She told some co-workers about the ideas in my book and they got interested and wanted to learn more. The secretary later asked her group VP to do an employee development workshop on the topic. The VP had heard that others were interested so they invited me to lead them in some of the exercises.

You would be surprised how many other people share your desire to work spiritually. Don't be afraid to tell others about the kind of work environment you would like to create.

As I began writing this book, I was overwhelmed by the receptivity people had to the idea of spirituality in the workplace. It speaks to a deeper yearning people are feeling to have jobs that feed them spiritually. Those people who want to work spiritually need to align themselves with organizations that allow them to be fully spiritual beings.

It may be, however, that you are in such a toxic work environment or soul-deadening job that you need to find work elsewhere. In so doing, seek out a company that allows for greater growth and wholeness. No matter what your job, there are always some steps you can take right where you are to bring spirituality to your work. Perhaps you are just the one to help your workplace become more spiritual.

PARADIGM SHIFT

Imagine being in a work environment where people are understanding of one another, forgiving of each other's shortcomings, and compassionate towards one another. Would your workgroup or department work better in this type of environment than how it works now? People generally agree that this type of work environment would be one where performance would be greater, and personal growth could happen. Office politics, rumor mills, and back-stabbing drain people's time, energy, and creativity. Intentionally spiritual environments build people's energy and support people's growth.

Though the phrase "paradigm shift" has been part of the popular business lexicon for most of the 1990s, it was presented by Thomas Kuhn in the 1970s in reference to shifts in scientific theories and the result these shifts had on how we understand our world. In his book *The Structure of Scientific Revolutions*, Kuhn presents shifts in paradigms as radical changes in the prevailing perspective of the era. Paradigmatic shifts lead to completely new ways of living and thinking about the world. Moving from pre-Copernican to the Copernican view of the position of the earth in relation to the sun is one such example. Darwin's theory of evolution resulted in another paradigmatic shift. Each shift challenged the dominant view of its time.

Similarly, what I am proposing is a paradigmatic shift for organizations, whether they are businesses, government agencies, or civic organizations. We must change how we view organizations and work to see them in a spiritual light. Organizations that follow the new paradigm are what I am calling Higher Consciousness Organizations.

While many leading businesses today already adopt some characteristics of Higher Consciousness Organizations, the essence of creating the "new organizations of the twenty-first century" comes in radically reframing why organizations exist and how organizations operate. Higher Consciousness Organizations operate from a spiritual set of principles and different fundamental premises. These principles and basic assumptions follow a spiritual perspective. When organizations tap into the spiritual depths of their members and support their spiritual development, they can harness unimagined resources.

All organizations are built on basic assumptions and beliefs about how best to operate. Higher Consciousness Organizations are based on a new paradigm, a new way of viewing work relationships and organizing. They are based on a different framework and belief system than traditional organizations. In the final chapter, I will describe how the new paradigm translates into how work is structured and conducted in Higher Consciousness Organizations.

The assumptions and perspectives that different organizations adopt under Old vs. New paradigms are presented below. [5]

Old Paradigm	New Paradigm
Economic Value of Organizing	Spiritual Human Value of Organizing
Work is Contractual	Work is a Calling and Service
Employee Defined by Job Roles	Employee Understood from Level of Spiritual Development
Scarcity Mentality	Abundance Mentality
Independent-Dependent View of World	Interdependent View of World
Uncertainty is Threat	Uncertainty is Opportunity
Product and Services Based	Values and Principles Based
Organization as Functions	Organization as Community
Command and Control	Participation, Involvement and Trust
Fear Based	Love Based
Finite Power	Infinite Power

The first three paradigm differences have been discussed in earlier chapters. According to this new paradigm, the human endeavor is viewed as a spiritual journey that occurs in work as in other areas of life. Similarly, organizations are a collective arena for that spiritual work to be accomplished. Therefore, the value of organizing is no longer based on economic units obtained but on spiritual development and growth.

When we carefully examine the question of "Whom does the Grail serve?" we look for those served beyond the general manager, senior partners, and major stockholders. As one person said in a client session, "In my old job we were all working so that the senior partners could get a new Mercedes. That didn't motivate us too long." When people feel they are serving a higher purpose, whether it is to grow spiritually on your own or with others, you will find a greater sense of purpose, motivation, and inspiration.

Work in the new paradigm is seen as a calling or service rather than merely a contractual agreement to do some unit of work for some unit of benefit. Work is offered from a place of Love and growth, done with a sense of larger purpose and service to God. The primary interest is in personal growth, not material gains. In this way, people come together in organizations and do their work with enlightened self-interest, not purely economic or material self-interest.

When work is seen as a calling or service, employees are not defined by their roles within their organization, but by their ability to serve others spiritually. This sense of service draws from one's emotional and spiritual development. In many organizations, people play unofficial roles of coach, advocate, ombudsperson, counselor, mediator, etc. Usually these people take on these roles informally with others. Often these people possess deeper spiritual and/or emotional characteristics that are reflected in their integrity, trustworthiness, or maturity.

ABUNDANCE AND OPPORTUNITY

Another aspect of the new paradigm is that organizations do not hold a scarcity mentality of themselves. They see themselves as offering abundant ideas, energy, and skills.
A scarcity mentality builds barriers and prevents people from seeing new possibilities. Abundance mentality is based on the notion that giving begets more, not less. This is particularly true for power and leadership. The more you give power and leadership to others, the more respect and commitment you

get in return, which builds your own power and leadership. The win-lose fixed pie model is based on a scarcity mentality. The abundance mentality looks for win-win options in all circumstances. In new paradigm thinking, creating abundance means being a co-creator with Divine or natural forces to bring more abundance.

In the new spiritual paradigm, we unleash the potential in others and move people past the limited view many hold of themselves. In this way, people see that energy can be created from within and can work to build on that energy. They see the infinite energy and power within them and among their co-workers to create what they desire.

An abundance mentality is most helpful in times of impending downsizing. In 1992, Chevron faced the prospect of letting go many talented engineers, while at the same time they needed differently skilled engineers at other plants. Rather than focusing on the scarcity of declining revenue and shortage of specific skilled workers, they looked within to retrain many employees to fill the other positions. Nearly 80% of the workers who were initially targeted to lose their jobs where retrained and repositioned in another plant. The company saved money by not needing to offer severance packages and conducting national job searches, and employees were provided another opportunity to expand their skills and have meaningful work. This is an example of senior executives using an abundance mentality to see the opportunities presented rather than having the scarcity mentality limit their options. [6]

At the same time as creating abundance, the new spiritual paradigm for organizations highlights the interconnectedness of all life. Therefore, one cannot create abundance by stealing it, literally or symbolically, from others. To do damage to another as a means to create your own abundance does damage ultimately. This applies to natural earth resources as well. Taking unlimited resources from the earth and not replenishing them only does damage in the end. New paradigm thinkers recognize the interdependence of people and the planet, and thus work with that understanding to create abundance that can be sustained. Abundance here does not mean greed or wastefulness. Taking energy from others or doing damage in other ways to another for your selfish gain is not part of working in the new paradigm.

By recognizing abundance rather than scarcity, we see uncertainty as an opportunity for growth and creation. Rather than seeing uncertainty yielding more scarcity, we recognize that uncertainty provides a challenge and opportunity to bring something into existence that may not have yet been created. That creation can come in a physical form such as a new product or in a developmental form such as someone learning a new way to communicate or work with others.

> *Some men see things as they are and say 'Why?' I dream things that never were and say 'Why not?'*
>
> – George Bernard Shaw

Many companies that do well believe they will be great and will make it big. The material flows from thoughts, words, and energy. If people put forth the intention of using energy for growth and abundance and ask for greater guidance in doing so, the co-creation process occurs.

Uncertainty from changes in management or job changes often results in people digging in or circling the wagons, anticipating the worst will happen. We must take great care to present change as an opportunity for new growth. Even when management and leadership change, core values and principles of the organization must be maintained. It is crucial for organizations to develop their core principles with the participation and acceptance of all members. By doing so, people will model these principles in their work. In current organizations, such principles include honesty, respect, and cooperation. More emphasis has been given in the 1990s to principles of personal character such as integrity and authenticity. The core principles of working spiritually in the new paradigm include principles such as forgiveness, redemption, compassion, and grace.

Change is often unsettling and threatening when people feel vulnerable. Much of this vulnerability comes from a scarcity mentality within ourselves, worried that we don't have enough security, job skills, or other opportunities. People also feel vulnerable because in most organizations employees are valued only as interchangeable commodities in the roles they serve. People begin to believe that a higher purpose is served when organizations hold the view that people are spiritual beings, that there is abundance within the company, and that the spiritual principles will be honored. Thus, people are more willing to cooperate for a greater good and build upon the energy each brings to his work.

TRUTHFUL COMMUNITY

According to the new paradigm, organizations see themselves as a community, an integrated whole rather than a combination of separate divisions, department, or functions. From this community perspective, they see that what affects one department will affect the whole organization. Thus, organizations don't set up competition between departments or foster rivalries between divisions because that does damage to the whole. Many ill or dysfunctional organizations see themselves as disjointed pieces. If there is cancer in one part of your body, do you ignore it because it hasn't spread to the rest of your body? In this holistic new paradigm framework if there is a problem in one division, it needs to be addressed in order for the rest of the organization to be healthy.

The work of M. Scott Peck described earlier is helpful for understanding what is required to be in community with one another. Maintaining community takes a tremendous amount of effort and dedication because community can break apart and revert to previous phases when new stresses emerge. Thus, the new paradigm involves organizations taking a long term perspective of themselves. They know that investing the time to reach a sense of community and rebuild community when it is shaken will pay off in the long run. We must pay more attention to the long term vision than the short term gains.

World economies are always so tenuous and we are subject to so many losses in life, but a compassionate attitude is something that we can always carry with us.

— the Dalai Lama

Too many companies look to restructuring and downsizing as a quick fix to their performance problems. However, in this effort to boost profits, many high performing employees leave along with the lesser performing ones. *Nearly one third of all companies that downsize don't reach profit objectives within two years of the downsizing, and nearly two thirds have to downsize again.*[7] The downsizing response has not worked as a quick fix to productivity problems.[8]

Fundamental human relationships and personal growth can't be redressed with quick fix solutions to solve deeper organizational problems. Poor customer service, low motivation, and poor teamwork require more time and effort than are usually given. Solutions must be ones that speak deeply to the individuals involved to have any meaningful or lasting impact. Unfortunately, too few people in organizations are willing to ask the tough questions to get at the deeper issues involved. Most organizations have the culture of being polite rather than seeking the truth. Seeking the truth may push people beyond their comfortable zones. But as the story of Perceval and the Holy Grail teaches us, we must be willing to ask the tough questions.

Finally, and most importantly, in the new paradigm, actions are based on the criteria – "what would Love do now?" In the new paradigm, decisions aren't based on fear (usually derived from a scarcity model). Instead, there is a connection to the loving, guiding presence of God. When we open ourselves to accepting and co-creating with God, our work is based on love. Our work relationships grow deeper and more loving as we accept our calling to work spiritually.

EXERCISES

1. What aspects of the Old vs. New paradigms are found in your organization? How can you move your organization, department, or work group towards accepting the new paradigm?

2. What experiences have you had with the loving presence of God? How have you opened yourself to allow the Grace of God to enter your life? Recreate that openness at work for a week and see what changes occur.

17

BECOMING A HIGHER CONSCIOUSNESS ORGANIZATION

Spirituality is an experience. It's your level of consciousness
that determines what that experience will be.

– Martin Rutte

WHY BECOME A HIGHER CONSCIOUSNESS

ORGANIZATION?

Government agencies, businesses, and non-profit organizations are faced with new challenges to be more responsive to their constituent or customer needs. Change and continual improvement is required of all organizations. Corporate and government downsizing in the 1980s and 1990s

253

have taught people that the old social contract between individuals and organizations no longer applies. Hard work and loyalty no longer mean job security if organizational members aren't able to meet the changing demands.

A natural reaction in such turbulent times is to look out for your own self-interest. But a democracy and free market capitalist system will not succeed based purely on individual self interest. Centuries ago, farmers used to share a common area for grazing their cows and sheep. Inevitably, it became apparent that overgrazing would destroy the commons and no one's livestock would thrive. Thus, farmers learned that if everyone acted out of pure self interest, all would lose.

The solution to the dilemma of the commons was to share the land and rotate when different livestock would graze. In this way, individual success was determined by collective co-operation. Social interest is needed to ensure our health and growth, both individually and collectively.

The Russian stock market crash in 1998 demonstrates the devastating effects of investors looking out only for them-selves. The repercussions of the Russian financial roulette were felt from Europe to Wall Street to Brazil. Social unrest results when individual self interest is the primary motivator. In a global economy the human toil is massive. As one com-mentator put it, "Boris Yeltsin went to bed drunk and the people of Brazil woke up with a hangover."[1]

The organizations that see their future in a global economy know that they must be ready and able to handle change. Greater flexibility comes from replacing old paradigms of managing and old ways of operating with a new paradigm for organizations. The significant downsizing required by such stalwarts of the twentieth century as IBM, General Electric, and AT&T are evidence that new ways of working are needed. Organizations that rely on the traditional way of making and implementing decisions through command and control structures have failed. The new paradigm focuses on a collective, win-win approach for personal growth and contribution to a Higher Purpose.

Many organizations are currently moving in the direction of becoming Higher Consciousness Organizations in their efforts to empower people, to see their staff as their greatest assets, and to motivate them intrinsically to perform at a higher level. Companies are bringing in speakers and consultants like David Whyte to talk about spirituality as a way to help them be more creative. The next step is to examine spirituality as a way to help groups work more effectively and to help employees find their gifts through their work. Doing so enhances greater personal development and fosters greater organizational effectiveness in the ever-changing, and increasingly competitive, global economy.

In the next section these fundamental ideas are examined:

1. Organizations are arenas in which personal development occurs.

2. People are capable of growing best in spiritually supportive environments.

3. Work is service.

4. People work from their own level of spiritual development.

5. Working spiritually taps deeper capacity and creates positive synergy.

BASIC PREMISES OF HIGHER CONSCIOUSNESS ORGANIZATIONS

In order to become a Higher Consciousness Organization you must shift your paradigm to see the world in a new way. As you see work and organizations operating from a spiritual perspective, the following premises become clear:

1. **ORGANIZATIONS ARE ARENAS IN WHICH PERSONAL DEVELOPMENT OCCURS.**

   The emphasis of Higher Consciousness Organizations is to develop people first and foremost; profits are a byproduct, not a driving force of these organizations. Therefore, Higher Consciousness Organizations are fundamentally learning organizations that reward personal growth for long term productivity.

2. **PEOPLE ARE CAPABLE OF GROWING BEST IN SPIRITUALLY SUPPORTIVE ENVIRONMENTS.**

   Higher Consciousness Organizations create environments that nurture and promote members' capacity to grow by providing opportunities for personal growth. Higher Consciousness Organizations structure work and work groups to help peak experiences occur, to promote "Aha" insights to happen, to move people towards their Highest Purpose, and to help people see their work as a contribution for a Higher Good.

3. **WORK IS SERVICE.**

   When work is viewed as a calling to serve, the temptation to work for prestige, power, ego, or material gains is minimized. Organizational members see their personal growth as an outreach of service in whatever way is necessary for a higher good. Serving a higher good means giving up turf guarding, hidden agendas, or personal material gains at the expense of others.

Service involves helping others in their growth and giving others opportunities to develop their skills. People develop their spiritual skills as well as mental, emotional, and technical skills through service. In doing service to others, you expand your own capacity to offer compassionate understanding and loving kindness.

4. **People work from their own level of spiritual development.**

Higher Consciousness Organizations see spiritual and emotional development as part of an organization's diversity. Higher Consciousness Organizations work with people at whatever level of development they are. As people grow spiritually, some aspect of their job will need to change to reflect those changes and allow further growth to happen.

People will serve in a variety of ways using the myriad of gifts they have to offer. They need to be given the opportunity to be themselves so that their gifts can come forth.

5. **Working spiritually taps deeper capacity and creates positive synergy.**

People can either drain energy from others or add energy to others. Team performance depends on members' ability to offer energy to each other. Taking energy from others is a result of feeling powerless, discouraged, injured, or not in control. As groups learn to recognize and develop ways in which energy is shared, they then combine their collective energy for greater performance.

Higher Consciousness Organizations work to coordinate this synergy for maximum performance.

One caveat is needed here. Focusing on spirituality merely as a means for greater profits will diminish the efforts. I would hate to see spirituality in the workplace as the latest management "program" of the month. Any efforts to inject spirituality into the workplace must come with the pure intention of supporting people's spiritual growth along their unique path for greatness. As an employee at Southwest Airlines put it, "Here we support people and use programs. At most companies they support programs and use people." This is an important distinction to keep in mind as spirituality at work enters into mainstream thinking. Spirituality should not be introduced as another way to use people.

BECOMING A HIGHER CONSCIOUSNESS ORGANIZATION

Working spiritually means a convergence of new ways of operating at the individual, group, and organizational levels. Becoming a Higher Consciousness Organization requires people to behave based on universal spiritual principles such as authenticity, compassion, forgiveness, service, *and* it requires organizations to support these principles. Most of us know we should act according to these principles, but have a hard time doing it. It takes practice and effort to learn how to work spiritually and it takes organizational environments and cultures to support that practice. In many cases, personal and organizational healing must be done so that people can work together in a spirit of Love.

A necessary first step is to build individual and organizational commitment to living and working spiritually. We must see ourselves as serving a higher purpose than immediate gains for us as individuals or for our organizations. The driving inner force must be to develop our Highest Self. We must develop that "light within" to guide us in times of conflict, stress, or confusion. This inner light must be sustained and supported to be a clear beacon for all our actions.

No enterprise can exist for itself alone. It ministers to some great need, it performs some great service not for itself, but for others.

— Calvin Coolidge

Shifting from where most organizations are now to becoming Higher Consciousness Organizations will require individuals to accept their role as change agents and for organizations to see how they will benefit from doing so. People who are effective change agents to develop Higher Consciousness Organizations will not only lift others up to be the highest they can be, but will find ways to create change so that their organization supports this growth as well.

Higher Consciousness Organizations have characteristics that best promote personal and organizational change. Higher Consciousness Organizations are able to change themselves as many times as necessary to meet external demands because they take as their working assumption that they are learning organizations. Learning doesn't take place where people are defensive, self-serving at others' expense, or quick to judge one another. Instead, learning environments are ones in which people are forgiving of others' imperfections and offer compassionate understanding. In this type of environment, people are able to experiment and learn from mistakes. In an affirming environment, people are able to honestly evaluate what actions were done and find clarity on how to address problems, rather than covering up or passing blame. In a spiritually aware and focused environment, personal change and growth happen while resistance to change is reduced.

HOW HIGHER CONSCIOUSNESS ORGANIZATIONS OPERATE

Currently accepted rules for structuring work (i.e., linear chain of command) come from Max Weber's proposed bureaucracy as the ideal form of organizations. However, as people and work have evolved, these traditional forms of structure and coordination no longer apply. Below is a list of characteristics found in Traditional vs. Higher Consciousness Organizations.[2]

Traditional Organizations	Higher Consciousness Organizations
Control by Hierarchy	Involvement by Connections & Relationships
Efficiency Focused	Growth Focused
Accountability to Others	Responsibility for Self
Individualistic Focus	Synergistic Focus
Competitive Relationships	Cooperative Relationships
Differences = Tension	Diversity = Growth and Opportunities
Hierarchy = Separation and Isolation	Inclusivity = Acceptance
Corporate Vision is Bottom Line	Corporate Vision is Holistic (People, Profit, and Society)
Structure and Rule Focused	Learning and Renewal Focused
Norms to be Nice and Polite	Norms to have Spiritual Love and Respect
Paternalistic Management	Stewardship Management

Traditional organizations get work done through command and control mechanisms. Higher Consciousness Organizations focus on creativity, synergy, and growth. They stay true to the common thread of universal yearnings and growth conditions (trust, honesty, forgiveness, and compassion). Even with different ideas, backgrounds, and work styles, people can come together on such basic ideals. Teamwork and flatter organizational structures are already moving in this direction.

In doing research for this book, I visited a marketing company that knew how to pool people's talents effectively. The Center for Creative Leadership had assessed this company's organizational characteristics, particularly as it related to teamwork and creativity. Their level of synergy was off the charts. The company staff had rated the company as being far more creative than the staff saw themselves individually. When they put their minds together they created new energy and better ideas. Their synergy was a result of the staff feeling secure enough with one another to put out crazy ideas and build on them. The whole office building was designed for creativity and fun, with objects hanging from the walls and numerous toys and games used as essential work tools.

This company believes that each person has something to offer the company in his or her own way. One example of this is at their annual planning retreat where *all* the staff attend. At their 1998 planning retreat they set their growth goals for the following year and then exceeded those annual goals by May 1999.

Higher Consciousness Organizations are a place where people find their wholeness, where they use their gifts and talents, and live authentically. By seeing people at different stages in their personal spiritual growth, the organization recognizes the diversity of its members. People are respected for who they are at whatever level of growth they are at, and are asked to serve as best they can. The organization builds on the member's diverse gifts and stages of development for all to grow. Organizational members are honored for their gifts, however great or small, and treated as divine loving beings. Higher Consciousness Organizations recognize their members as Spiritual Beings rather than Human Doings.

Personal Growth is Top Priority

The more we can see each other as teachers and nurturers of our personal spiritual development, the more we help move each other along. There is no need for judgment or labeling of people who are not at the same level or moving as quickly as others. People follow their own path with various levels of challenges. We don't know their barriers or blocks that need to be removed for further growth. However, we can offer compassion, support, and encouragement to help them get through the barriers and blocks when they are stuck, and celebrate with them as they move to healthier ways of being.

Taking the time to work on co-worker relations is important for organizational effectiveness and for personal growth. Extensive turnover and absenteeism are often indicators of deeper levels of conflict or dissatisfaction that need to be addressed. Turnover impacts the bottom line, yet rarely are human resource matters factored into a company's performance rating. Luckily, some companies understand that their employees are their greatest asset and include Human Resources in their strategic planning.[3]

In the early 1990s, Jeffrey Swartz, CEO of Timberland, began an initiative of providing company time for employees to participate more in their community. Many employees were already volunteering in their churches and local schools. Jeffrey understood the value of such work and institutionalized it at Timberland.

When Timberland faced major liquidity problems in 1995, he told his employees the only way the company was going to succeed was by everyone giving 100% of themselves. But he knew they wouldn't give 100% to the company if the company didn't honor and recognize the employees 100%. During this crisis period, rather than eliminate the amount of time people were given to be engaged in their community, he *doubled* the amount of time they were given. In this way, he recognized that what was important to the employees would be brought back to the company, that is, a belief in giving to a larger community for a greater good.[4]

The company turned around its sales and accounts receivable, and grew stronger financially over the next two years. Besides the financial success achieved, the employees felt a greater sense of commitment to the company because the company recognized that work must be integrated with family and community obligations.

PERFORMANCE REVIEWS, PROMOTIONS, AND TRANSITIONS

One opportunity to provide encouragement and support is in the performance review process. Unfortunately, performance reviews are seen as a time of great anxiety. They are used ostensibly to determine salary raises based on performance levels. However, most salary raises are given across the board or are based on seniority. The performance review process is generally a political one that doesn't allow for constructive feedback to improve performance or personal growth.[5] This time could be valuable to reflect on those opportunities for growth and how well they were used.

Many companies have adopted the philosophy of "hire for attitude, train for skills." This focus in recruiting workers for their personal attitudes and character exemplifies the shift taking place in businesses. It is no longer enough to have the technical skill set without the personal skills too. But even attitude must be more clearly defined. High personal integrity is different from having a "good attitude." Character development is more than being cheerful and coming to work on time (though these are also important). It means being authentic and honest to recognize your shortfalls and being willing to work on them, as well as being forgiving of others' shortfalls and having compassionate understanding to help others develop into more caring and respectful people.

Higher Consciousness Organizations are places where people learn from relationships and grow individually and collectively. They are fluid such that people move in and out as necessary so that their learning moves to its next highest level. Similarly, HCOs understand the cyclical nature of life. No one can go full speed ahead all the time. Indeed, most people burn out physically or emotionally if they try to do so. Therefore, taking time out for reflection and rejuvenation is important. Companies that offer sabbaticals know how beneficial this time is for greater learning.

We enjoy the quality of the moment knowing that there will be enough time to do everything of importance, and we create a space for the universe to surprise us with magic.

– Tanis Helliwell

Adhering to a cyclical time frame of outward growth and inward reflection allows for a more natural flow of experiences. Most companies have retreats to review what they have accomplished and plan for the future. Unfortunately, most organizations provide this "time out" for only the top tier members. Too few organizations allow this reflective time for front line staff, yet they are the ones who may need to be recharged the most, and who can offer the best insights into what changes need to be made.

People who are discovering what they need or want in order to grow as part of their spiritual journey are able to grow most effectively in organizations that support that growth. Members of Higher Consciousness Organizations approach their organization as a place to learn and move to their next highest level of being. People may move on to other organizations when they have learned all they can where they are, while others may choose to stay and be a light for others. Higher Consciousness Organizations support people moving on to other jobs and other arenas for their growth. Southwest Airlines has a career development progression more similar to a lattice than a ladder. They recognize that people want to try new jobs even if it doesn't mean moving "up" in the company. HCOs specifically hire and promote people who can assist team members' personal growth to wholeness.

TRUST AND TEAMWORK

Higher Consciousness Organizations coordinate work through involvement, participation, and trust. As decision making is moved lower down in organizations, employees need to feel empowered and trusted to make those decisions. A key in any empowerment program is trust. If upper management doesn't trust front line staff to have good judgment and to use it appropriately, they will never give away power enough to make empowerment work. Likewise, if employees don't trust upper management to make decisions in their best interest they will never work cooperatively with management. The crux of all empowerment and decentralized team efforts is trust in groups across the organization.

Since trust is so important to the functioning of organizations, and yet is so scarce in most organizations, Higher Consciousness Organizations intentionally and repeatedly focus on building that trust. Rather than base decisions, policies, and procedures on fear (fear of change, fear of law suits, fear of scarcity), Higher Consciousness Organizations ensure that compassion, trust, and respect are abundant throughout the organization.

Trust and teamwork are critical elements to effective work and no organization can function well without it. Anyone who has tried to conduct a business transaction when there was no trust or tried to maintain a personal relationship knows that trust is an essential ingredient. When making any decision or implementing new ideas, the essential criteria must be – "will we build trust by doing this?"

Once trust is established, groups and teams can then function effectively. Groups make better decisions when they trust one another to work for the collective good. By looking for deeper truths, offering compassionate understanding of others' shortcomings, and making space for grace to enter, teams and whole departments function at a much higher level.

When we make the commitment to work spiritually, we see our work as an opportunity to grow spiritually through our encounters with others. In the daily interactions we can apply our spiritual practice and support others in their growth as well. Let me be clear that working spiritually doesn't mean forcing others to accept your particular religious belief. Working spiritually by serving others means helping others along *their* spiritual path. The effort Jeffrey Swartz took with his sales employee who was Muslim is such an example. Similarly, it's essential we accept that co-workers will follow a spiritual path in their own time. If people are not open to their own spiritual growth you can't make them pursue it. We must allow others their freedom to choose to work spiritually or not.

VISION AND LEADERSHIP

The corporate vision in Higher Consciousness Organizations is on serving a larger purpose and broader set of constituents. The Stakeholder approach of serving employees and society, in addition to stockholders, means profits are no longer the sole reason for being. Increasing the bottom line is not the sole corporate vision. Instead, taking a holistic vision, Higher Consciousness Organizations see that they stay in business to serve a larger purpose than making some people rich.

Ten years from now, we want magazines to write about GE as a place where people have the freedom to be creative, a place that brings out the best in everybody, an open, fair place where people have a sense that what they do matters, and where that sense of accomplishment is rewarded in both the pocketbook and the soul.

— Jack Welch,
CEO General Electric

Internal management and operating practices are based on spiritual Love and respect. Higher Consciousness Organizations know they must demonstrate through their behavior a respect for the environment, for each other, and for the larger society (or countries where the company operates). This type of stewardship management is very different from the paternalistic management approach of traditional organizations.

In the paternalistic approach, management is seen as the big daddy who will provide for and protect employees in a father-knows-best approach. Front line employees don't assume responsibility or share decision making power in the belief that the upper executives are responsible for everything.

A traditional "hero" view of leadership holds where lower level employees look to the CEO or managers to do the right thing and don't see their roles as leaders with each other.

A stewardship management approach recognizes the responsibility for serving a higher purpose. Organizational leaders serve in tandem *with* those they serve. In a stewardship approach, organizational leaders share responsibility for their actions with their constituents. Employees throughout the organization are more involved in decision-making and share responsibility for the outcomes and effects of the organization. Leadership is shared and assumed by everyone. The "post-heroic" leadership model prevails, whereby no single person is expected to carry the day.

In Higher Consciousness Organizations (HCO), spiritually and emotionally mature people are formally recognized as leaders within their organization. Emotional intelligence must be rewarded and cultivated as much as traditional intelligence for organizations to prosper. One's character is just as important to cultivate and nurture as one's technical skills. Thus, personal character takes a high priority in HCOs and are developed and rewarded accordingly. Character goes beyond good interpersonal skills. Team skills such as cooperation are important, but personal character development goes much deeper. It gets to the essence of who you are and whether you will be honest, trustworthy, or compassionate. These character issues must take a front seat for organizations to thrive in the future.

Spiritually developed leaders have as part of their job assignments the task of helping others grow and mature so that they can work better with others. These leaders may not be selected for their technical skills but more for their emotional skills and character development. These high character leaders put greater emphasis on helping the organization nurture and support member's personal growth than on helping accomplish a technical task. They are role models and facilitators for applying the spiritual principles that organization members agree are important to practice and uphold. These leaders are recognized and cultivated throughout the organization, not just at the top.

SOUTHWEST AIRLINES DEMONSTRATES A NEW WAY TO WORK

Though executives at Southwest Airlines (SWA) would probably not use the phrase "Higher Consciousness Organization" to describe Southwest, the company does exhibit many HCO characteristics. They focus on their people first and foremost. By cultivating their people to be the best they can be, the organization performs well. They believe in growing their people to their fullest and allowing them to bring the wholeness of who they are to their work. People come before profits is not just a marketing slogan, it is a reality in this company.

Their "People Strategy Top 10 List" is as follows:

1. Give people freedom to be themselves

2. Hire for attitude, Train for skill

3. Provide a learning environment

4. Promote from within

5. Don't keep people who don't fit the culture

6. Communicate, Communicate, Communicate

7. Avoid Elitism, Kill Bureaucracy

8. Be Flexible, Forgive Mistakes

9.   Give Awards, Celebrate Everything

10.   Encourage People to act like Owners

I had the opportunity to visit Southwest Airlines, to watch them in action, and to talk to their staff. Walking onto a plane or entering the corporate offices in Dallas, Texas (intentionally located at Love Field) you immediately feel the energy and enthusiasm of the people who make up Southwest Airlines. They love their jobs. It shows not only by their "positively outrageous" customer service, but also in their financial performance. While other major airlines were falling off the radar in the 1980s and 90s, Southwest was the only US airline to turn a profit

> *I want to compete in the marketplace not in the workplace.*
>
> – Herb Kelleher

every year since 1973. It has doubled in size every five years since it began. All this success came with 80% of their workforce belonging to a union.

Southwest Airlines has been featured for their unconventional ways of operating in national magazines, prime time news, and the popular book, *Nuts!*. In 1998, *Fortune* magazine rated Southwest the best place to work.

Southwest wouldn't have grown as fast as it did if employees didn't believe in a common goal. While profit sharing is an important piece of keeping a common goal, it is certainly not the only way. Southwest won the "Triple Crown" award for quality performance four years in a row, from 1992 to 1995. No airline had ever won five Triple Crowns. Everyone caught the enthusiasm to try to be the first company to do so. When they won it in 1996, they had a "Gimme Five" award to nominate staff from across the country to go to pick up the plane in Seattle designed just for the occasion. On the overhead luggage compartments in the plane was engraved the name of *every* employee who worked in the company at the time. They all owned the accomplishment.

The company actively feeds the corporate culture of fun, love, and passion. They have "People Week" at offices all across the country to inspire and motivate workers throughout the year. Their 25th anniversary slogan was "25 years of Luv." Herb Kelleher has said "the company is bound by love more than by fear" and emphasizes that people "smile because we want to not because we have to."

You have to sign people up for a cause, not just give them a job.

– Colleen Barrett

The joy and playfulness of the company is exemplified by the CEO Herb Kelleher, but it permeates throughout the company. In fact, several people bristled at the question about what would happen to Southwest after Herb retires. From Herb's right-hand person, Colleen Barrett, on down, the staff believe Southwest's culture will continue after Herb retires because the employees are committed to keeping it.

Colleen Barrett formed Culture Committees throughout the company to "ensure the Southwest spirit is shared and nourished." They solicit people from different branch offices to be on the committee for two years. The committee meets three times a year for 8 hours at headquarters and then works in subcommittees to implement the ideas. They are all required to take three field trips a year to visit other offices. Staff do this *on their own time*! They do so because it is important to them to keep the culture alive.

Colleen believes, "You have to sign people up for a cause, not just give them a job." She wants people to go home and look themselves in the mirror and say "I had fun today." She believes its important to "tell people the negatives as well as the success so they believe you. You have to constantly share the truth with people but your people have to trust you."

The human resource and marketing staff speak of the company's passionate pursuit of fun. They keep that fun culture alive through numerous and creative employee awards such as "Walking the Talk" for leadership in demonstrating that fun and results go together and for sharing their passion. Another award "Heroes of Heart" goes to a team or department who are the unsung heroes behind the scenes. This award is given on Valentine's day. SWA created little cards with short sayings that employees can give to a co-worker. These are called "LUV pats" to help cheer someone up in difficult times or congratulate someone on a job well done.

If we lose the esprit de corp, the spirit of the culture – we lose our most competitive advantage.

– Herb Kelleher

Southwest Airlines epitomizes the belief in abundance. Instead of trying to win a piece of a limited market share of airline flyers, they believed the pie could expand. And they were right. They reduced their air fares to allow people to fly who had never flown before. When they started, only a small percent of Americans had flown before. In 1999, in large part due to Southwest Airlines reaching out to new customers, a majority of Americans fly. One of their corporate values is freedom – allowing people the freedom to fly so that it isn't just a privilege for the few.

At the Southwest headquarters there are slogans, pictures, and awards everywhere that expresses the principles, beliefs, and culture of the company. Posters of their "warrior spirit" motto hang in prominent places to remind people of the values and commitment to service required at Southwest. Several internal company slogans and mottoes that build a spiritually supportive work environment are: "Developing leaders that make a difference," "Pursue Love before Technique," and "Take your work seriously but don't take yourself too seriously."

Their University 4 People is one of the most impressive training and development department I've seen. Their goal is "to awaken the child-like spirit in us and ignite the curiosity of fire." They believe that "humor and creativity go hand in hand," and strive to turn "ha-ha's into a-has." Their new hire training called "You, Southwest and Success" has sections that deal with personal and company values, the history of the company, and the importance of love and compassion in work. Beyond the new hire training, which everyone goes through in their first 30 days, they offer 12 different classes, many offered on company time, for people interested in improving their skills. Several classes are designed for people who advance to supervisory positions to develop their leadership skills.

When employees pass their six month probation they get a pin to recognize the transition. Co-workers give a little cheer or acknowledgment to celebrate being part of the Southwest family. They have a saying "give me some love" when someone wants to be specially recognized. From their personnel handbook, called "Guideline for Leaders," to their "Wall of People" at corporate headquarters, it is apparent that they put people before profits. Their crazy publicity events and riotous annual dinners demonstrate they dare to be different and succeed by having fun.

Summary

Higher Consciousness Organizations are shaped by those who are willing to work from a place of wholeness, meaning, and connection. When more people become committed to working spiritually, more Higher Consciousness Organizations will develop. Moving from fear to compassionate understanding, loving kindness and Divine Love in most organizations is a tough challenge. And yet the payoff is immense. Ultimately, organizations that pay attention to Love build trust and foster personal growth. Compassionate understanding and forgiveness are essential for all healthy working relationships.

If this type of work environment speaks to you as a place where you would like to spend most of your waking hours, perhaps you are ready to help transform your organization into a Higher Consciousness Organization. HCOs have a different reason for being than traditional organizations. Higher Consciousness Organizations view the world and their purpose according to a different paradigm, a spiritual one. Through this new paradigm of work and organizations, we learn to live fully and more meaningfully, and ultimately we become more intentional spiritual beings.

EXERCISES

1. Review your organization and determine what aspects are consistent with Traditional vs. Higher Consciousness Organization characteristics.

    a. Which of the characteristics of HCOs seem most similar to how your organization operates?

    b. Which aspects are more like traditional organizations and not likely to change any time soon?

    c. Focusing on those characteristics that are most similar to HCOs, how can you get your organization, department, or division to be more intentional about operating in this way?

2. What people in your organization serve as caretakers, coaches, advocates? Are these roles formally recognized by your organization? What could your organization do to promote these roles or give it greater importance?

BIBLIOGRAPHY

Below are books and articles that have inspired my thinking or served as resources for this book. They are not the entire list of books that have informed my work. I offer these references for your review and greater learning.

Argyris, Chris, "Good Communication That Blocks Learning" in *Harvard Business Review*, July-Aug. 1994, 77-85.

Bach, Richard, *Illusions: The Adventures of a Reluctant Messiah*, Delacorte Press, NY, 1977.

Bolles, Richard, N. *What Color is Your Parachute: A Practical Manual for Job-Hunters and Career Changes*, Ten Speed Press, Berkeley, CA, 1991 edition.

Bolles, Richard, N. *The Three Boxes of Life and How to Get Out of Them*, Ten Speed Press, Berkeley, CA, 1978.

Campbell, Joseph, *Myths to Live By*, Bantam Books, NY, 1972.

Canfield, Jack et. al., *Chicken Soup for the Soul at Work*, Health Communications Inc., Deerfield Beach, FL, 1996.

Chapell, Tom, *The Soul of a Business: Managing for Profit and the Common Good*, Bantam Books, NY, 1993.

Chödrön, Pema, *Start Where You Are: A Guide to Compassionate Living*, Shambhala, Boston, 1994.

Chungliang, Al Huang and Lynch, Jerry, *Thinking Body, Dancing Mind: Tao Sports for Extraordinary Performance in Athletics, Business and Life*, Bantam Books, NY, 1994.

Covey, Stephen, *The Seven Habits of Highly Effective People*, Simon and Schuster, NY, 1989.

Covey, Stephen, *Principle-Centered Leadership*, Simon and Schuster, NY, 1990.

(The) Dalai Lama and Cutler, Howard C., *The Art of Happiness: A Handbook for Living*, Riverhead Books, NY, 1998.

Davidson, Let *Wisdom at Work: The Awakening of Consciousness in the Workplace*, Larson Publ., NY, 1998.

Dreikurs, Rudolf, *Fundamentals of Adlerian Psychology*, Alfred Adler Institute, Chicago, IL, 1949/1989.

Easwaran, Eknath, "Working in Freedom" in *Yoga International*, May/June 1995, 22-27.

Fields, Rick et. al., (Editors) *Chop Wood, Carry Water: A Guide to Finding Spiritual Fulfillment in Everyday Life*, Jeremy Tarcher Inc., Los Angeles, 1984.

French, W. & Bell, C. *Organization Development: Behavioral Science Interventions for Organizational Improvement*, Prentice Hall, Englewood Cliffs, NJ, 1995 (5th Ed.).

Fox, Matthew, "Redefining Work" in *Yoga International,* May/June 1995, 29-33.

Fox, Matthew, *"The Reinvention of Work: A New Vision of Livelihood for Our Time*, HarperCollins, San Francisco, 1994.

Gandhi, Mohandas, *Gandhi An Autobiography: The Story of My Experiments with Truth*, Beacon Press, Boston, 1957.

Gawain, Shakti, *Creative Visualizations: Use The Power of Your Imagination to Create What You Want in Your Life*, New World Library, Novato, CA, 1995.

Goldman, Ari , *The Search for God at Harvard*, Ballantine Books, NY, 1992.

Hagan, Kay Leigh, *Prayers to the Moon: Exercises in Self Reflection*, HarperCollins, San Francisco, 1991.

Hanh, Thich Nhat, *Being Peace*, Parallax Press, Berkeley, CA, 1987.

Hanh, Thich Nhat, *The Miracle of Mindfulness: A Manual on Meditation*, Beacon Press, Boston, 1992.

Hawley, Jack, *Reawakening the Spirit at Work*, Simon and Schuster, NY, 1993.

Heider, John, *The Tao of Leadership: Leadership Strategies for a New Age*, Bantam Books, NY, 1986.

Helliwell, Tanis, *Take Your Soul to Work: Transform Your Life and Work*, Random House of Canada, 1999.

Jeffers, Susan, *Feel the Fear and Do It Anyway*, Fawcett Book Group, NY, 1998.

King, Martin Luther, *The Words of Martin Luther King, Jr.*, Newmarket Press, NY, 1983.

King, Serge Kahili, *Urban Shaman: A Handbook for Personal and Planetary Transformation based on the Hawaiian Way of the Adventurer*, Simon and Schuster, NY, 1990.

Kuhn, Thomas S., *The Structure of Scientific Revolutions*, University of Chicago Press, Chicago, 1970.

McCarthy, Kevin, *The On-Purpose Business: Doing More of What You Do Best More Profitably*, Pinon Press, Colorado Springs, CO, 1998.

Nair, Keshavan, *A Higher Standard of Leadership: Lessons from the Life of Gandhi*. Berret-Koehler Publishers, San Francisco, 1997.

Oldenburg, Ray, *The Great Good Place*, Paragon House Publ, St. Paul MN, 1991.

Osterberg, Rolf, *Corporate Renaissance: Business as an Adventure in Human Development*, Nataraj Press, Mill Valley, CA, 1993.

Peck, M. Scott, *The Different Drum: Community Making and Peace*, Simon and Schuster, NY, 1988.

Peck, M. Scott, *A World Waiting to Be Born: Civility Rediscovered*, Bantam Books, NY, 1994.

Pfeffer, Jeffrey, *The Human Equation: Building Profits by Putting People First*, Harvard Business School Press, Boston, 1998.

Quinn, Robert, *Deep Change: Discovering the Leader Within*, Jossey-Bass, San Francisco, 1996.

Ray, Michael and Rinzler, Alan (Eds.), *The New Paradigm in Business: Emerging Strategies for Leadership and Organizational Change*, Tarter Putnam, NY, 1993.

Schaef, Anne W. and Fassel, Diane, *The Addictive Organization*, Harper and Row, San Francisco, 1988.

Schein, Edgar H., *Organizational Culture and Leadership*, Jossey-Bass, San Francisco, 1987.

Schucman, Helen, *A Course in Miracles*, Foundation for Inner Peace, Viking Press, NY, 1996.

Senge, Peter M., *The Fifth Discipline: The Art and Practice of the Learning Organization*, Doubleday, NY, 1990.

Severance, John B., *Gandhi: Great Soul*, Clarion Books, NY, 1997.

Sinetar, Marsha, *Do What You Love, The Money Will Follow: Choosing Your Right Livelihood*, Dell Publ., NY, 1989.

Sinetar, Marsha, *To Build the Life You Want, Create the Work You Love*, St. Martin's Griffin, NY, 1996.

Storm, Hyemeyohsts, *Seven Arrows*, Ballantine Book, NY, 1972.

Toms, Michael and Justine, *True Work: Doing What You Love and Loving What You Do*, Bell Tower, NY, 1998.

Tzu, Lao (translated by John C. Wu), *Tao Teh Ching*, Shambhala Publ., Boston, 1990.

Tzu, Sun (translated by Thomas Cleary), *The Art of War*, Shambhala Publ., Boston, 1991.

Walsch, Neale D., *Conversations with God: An Uncommon Dialogue*, Vol. 1, Hampton Roads Publishing, VA, 1995.

Whyte, David, *The Heart Aroused: Poetry and the Preservation of the Soul in Corporate America*, Doubleday, NY, 1994.

Weber, Max, *The Protestant Ethic and the Spirit of Capitalism*, translation by Talcott Parsons first published 1930, reprinted by Routledge, London, 1992.

ENDNOTES

Chapter 2

[1] Here Right Livelihood is not meant to connote the Divine. The steps along the Eightfold Path are traditionally capitalized.

[2] Thanks to Bill Breeden for using this example, given as part of an ordination in 1998.

Chapter 4

[1] "Serving the Lord" in *Shalom: The Heritage of Judaism in Selected Writings*. Tina Hacker (ed.), 13.

[2] Told by Margret Stevens in *Prosperity is God's Idea*.

Chapter 5

[1] Matthew Fox, *The Reinvention of Work*, 300.

[2] Jerry Lynch, *Thinking Body*, xviii.

[3] Tannis Helliwell, *Take Your Soul to Work*, 33-34.

[4] Peter Alsop's presentation, National Association of Prevention Professionals and Advocates (NAPPA) Conference, Minneapolis, MN, 1992.

[5] Fox, 299.

Chapter 6

[1] Dr. Elizabeth Loftus has written about this in her book *Eyewitness Testimony*, Harvard University Press, 1979.

Chapter 7

[1] Ware Lecture, Unitarian Universalist General Assembly, Rochester NY, June 1986.

[2] M.L. King Jr., *The Words of Martin Luther King Jr.*, 65.

[3] Dalai Lama and Howard Cutler, *The Art of Happiness*, 301.

[4] Ibid., 79.

[5] Ibid., 78.

[6] Jack Hawley, *Reawakening the Spirit at Work*, 53.

Chapter 10

[1] "Inside the Chemically Dependent Marriage: Denial and Manipulation" in *Co-Dependency: An Emerging Issue*. Hollywood Beach, FL, Health Communications 1984.

[2] Ibid.

[3] Schaef and Fassel, *The Addictive Organization,* 1988.

Chapter 11

[1] Jim Braham, "The Spiritual Side: CEOs Speaking Up," *Industry Week,* Feb. 1999, 48-56.

[2] From video presentation by Bob Marx at the Second International Symposium on Spirituality and Business, March 1999, Boston.

[3] From the International Symposium on Spirituality and Business, March 2000, Boston.

[4] The following articles provide an overview of team performance and appropriate reward systems:

Bob Nelson, "Does One Reward Fit All?" *Workforce,* Feb. 1997, 67-70.

Perr Pascarella, "Compensating Teams," *Across the Board,* Feb. 1997, 16-22.

Chapter 12

[1] For example, Allan Drexler et. al. *The Team Performance Model,* NTL Institute, MD, 1988.

[2] Such books include *How to Work for a Jerk* by Robert Houchheiser, *Nasty People* by Jay Carter, and *The Gentle Art of Verbal Self Defense* by Suzette Elgin.

Chapter 14

[1] Interview by John Love, *Quest*, 1979, 104.

[2] Ibid.

Chapter 15

[1] B. Nelson, "The Care of the Un-Downsized," *Training and Development*, April 1997, 41-43.

Chapter 16

[1] "Companies Hit the Road Less Traveled," *Business Week*, June 5, 1995.

[2] "Oddball Courses," *Washington Post*, Nov. 29, 1998.

[3] "Can Generation X-ers Be Trained?" *Training and Development*, March 1997.

[4] I am indebted to Dr. Camille Wright Miller and Dr. Cindy Lindsay for their assistance in framing the contributions of Taylor and Weber.

[5] This paradigm shift was formulated by myself and two colleagues of the WestWind Institute, Dawn Oparah and Cindy Lindsay.

[6] "New Skills Equal New Opportunities," *Personnel Journal*, June 1996.

[7] Nelson, 41-43.

[8] Schneier et. al., "Companies' Attempts to Improve Performance While Containing Costs: Quick Fix versus Lasting Change," *Human Resource Planning*, 1992, 1-25.

Chapter 17

[1] *Frontline* segment, "The Crash" 1999.

[2] The characteristics of Higher Consciousness Organizations were developed during a retreat with my colleagues, Dawn Oparah and Cindy Lindsay. Concurrent to writing this book, Dr. Lindsay is writing a book on meaning in organizations. Several of the comparisons of Traditional vs. Higher Consciousness organizations are examined in her book as well.

[3] See articles such as G. Flynn, "Can't Get This Big without HR Deluxe," *Personnel Journal*, Dec. 1996, 47-53.

[4] From Swartz's presentation given at the Second International Symposium on Spirituality and Business, Boston MA, March 1999.

[5] Longenecker et. al., "Behind the Mask: The Politics of Employee Appraisal," *Academy of Management Executive*, *1*, 1987, 183-193.

About the Author

Dr. Linda Ferguson is president and owner of *New Paradigms Consulting,* a consulting firm specializing in organization development and personal mastery. Dr. Ferguson facilitates groups, leads retreats, and conducts workshops on effective communication, conflict resolution and group dynamics, leadership development, team building, strategic planning, and working spiritually. Her latest work is teaching the process of Transformational Empowerment ™.

Dr. Ferguson earned her Ph.D. from Indiana University (I.U.-Bloomington) in Organizational Behavior with a Masters also from I.U. studying Social Psychology. She has taught undergraduate and graduate courses in psychology and management at colleges in Indiana and Virginia. In 1994 she traveled abroad for six months to Asia, Australia, Israel and Europe. Dr. Ferguson resides in Roanoke Virginia and can be contacted through her website: www.lindajferguson.com

ISBN 155212498-3